KATHLEEN WATSON, MBA

NETPROFIT

Business Networking Without the Nerves

NET PROFIT © copyright 2007 by Kathleen Watson. All rights reserved. No part of this book may be reproduced in any form whatsoever, by photography or xerography or by any other means, by broadcast or transmission, by translation into any kind of language, nor by recording electronically or otherwise, without permission in writing from the author, except by a reviewer, who may quote brief passages in critical articles or reviews.

ISBN 10: 1-931945-71-3
ISBN 13: 978-1-931945-71-4

Library of Congress Catalog Number: 2007928392

Printed in the United States of America

First Printing: June 2007

11 10 09 08 07   5 4 3 2 1

Expert Publishing, Inc.
14314 Thrush Street NW,
Andover, MN 55304-3330

Andover, 1-877-755-4966
Minnesota www.expertpublishinginc.com

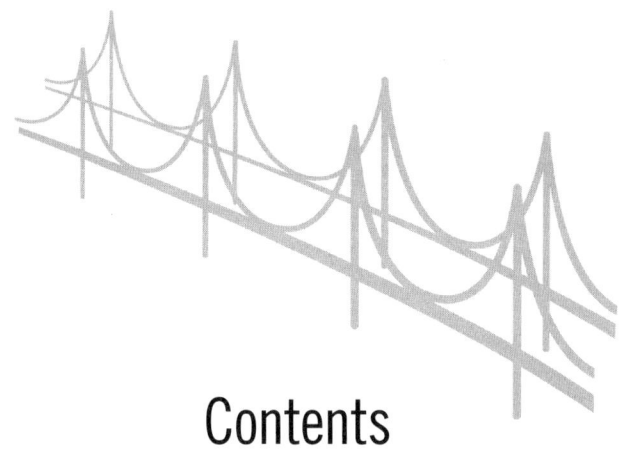

Contents

Acknowledgments..v
Introduction vii

1	What's Your NQ?	1
2	Non-Verbal Communication: Body Language	5
3	Non-Verbal Communication: Delivery	11
4	Verbal Communication.................................	17
5	Deciding Where to Invest Your Time, Money, and Energy......	21
6	Preparing for the Event	25
7	Behavior at the Event..................................	29
8	Effective Follow-Up	37
9	Networking for New College Graduates	43
10	Networking in Your Current Industry......................	51
11	Networking for a Move to a New Industry	55
12	Networking for Your Own Business.......................	59
13	Networking at Business Expos and Trade Shows	67
14	Pulling it All Together.................................	75

Appendix A: Scoring Your NQ Self-Assessment 77
Appendix B: Questions for Evaluating Prospective Membership Groups . 79
Appendix C: Informational Interview Data Sheet.................... 81
Appendix D: The Difference Between Blah and Brilliant 83
Appendix E: Additional Resources................................ 87
About the Author.. 88

Acknowledgments

I owe special thanks to a number of people:

Lauri Flaquer of Saltar Solutions, the exceptional marketing consultant who encouraged (one might even say nagged) me to share my ideas with others.

Sharron Stockhausen of Expert Publishing Inc., for being a wonderfully effective, educational, and compassionate editor.

Harry Stockhausen, also of Expert Publishing, for being a terrific hand holder.

And Joseph, my husband, for keeping our golden retrievers out of my hair while I worked on the book and for being one of the most encouraging people I've ever been privileged to know.

Introduction

Each of us networks on a daily basis. Whether we're looking for a personal or professional contact, we know that our friends and acquaintances are valuable resources for making important connections.

But networking presents a serious challenge for many business people. All too often a business owner will pay money to join an organization for purposes of networking, only to quit in disgust because "I didn't get anything out of my membership." Typically, such a missed opportunity could have been avoided if she had practiced more effective networking skills.

At one point or another I suspect I've made—and dealt with the consequences of—virtually all of the networking errors known to humankind. This means I've learned from experience not only myriad ways to do it wrong, but equally many ways to do it right. A more efficient (and less painful) way to learn is to observe those who seem to be natural networkers. If we can identify how the naturals think and act, then adopt those thoughts and behaviors, we're able to enjoy networking effectively on behalf of ourselves or others.

In the following pages, you'll get a chance to identify networking skills you already have in abundance, as well as those that could use some work, and then focus your attention on polishing the latter. This book was designed to be light on theory and heavy on practical tips—hence the workbook format. The more energy you put into completing the exercises in writing, and the more you *practice* the skills, the higher your return on the time and money you invest in networking.

Increasing Competence

Everyone travels through four distinct stages in learning any new skill, as shown in boxes one through four:

	Unconscious State of Mind	**Conscious State of Mind**
Incompetence	1. Unconscious Incompetence, or "Ignorance is Bliss": you don't know what you don't know	2. Conscious Incompetence, or "The V8 Moment": you smack yourself on the forehead because you realize what you don't know and commit to changing that situation
Competence	4. Unconscious Competence, or "The No-Brainer": your skill is so highly developed that you apply it without even thinking	3. Conscious Competence, or "Put Tab *A* Into Slot *B*": you've developed the desired skill and consciously, perhaps somewhat awkwardly, apply it

As you read through this book, you'll probably find that you're at different stages in different areas, and this will enable you to make informed decisions about allocating your time and energy. You can devote the most attention to the areas where you're unconsciously or consciously incompetent, you can spend some time refining skills in which you're consciously competent, and you can bask in the glow of unconscious competence in yet other areas.

Don't be surprised or dismissive if some of this information is old hat to you. Instead, if you hear yourself saying, "Well, I know *that*," ask yourself if you actually put that particular behavior *into practice*. Remember, it's *applied* knowledge that is power.

And a final note. Although this book can be used effectively by both men and women, I didn't want to play the "he or she" game throughout. Consequently, you'll find that all the pronouns are feminine, just to make reading easier and more consistent.

What's Your NQ?

Since nobody does everything perfectly, take the following self-assessment to determine your **N**etworking **Q**uotient and establish a baseline of your networking skills.

1. How do people tend to react to your handshake?
   a. with a warm smile and interest
   b. with a grimace of pain
   c. by releasing your hand as quickly as possible

2. What do you see the most of when speaking to someone at a networking event?
   a. your shoes
   b. other people around the room
   c. the face of the person you're speaking with

3. What type of comment do you hear most frequently at networking events?
   a. "Hi. Is this your first time attending one of these?"
   b. "Wow! It seems I see you everywhere I go."
   c. "I know I've seen you a couple of times, but I'm afraid I don't remember your name."

NET PROFIT

4. Say you've spoken with someone several times before at previous networking events. If she were to introduce you and your business to a third party, what would she say?
   a. she wouldn't know enough about you or your business to introduce you
   b. after a quick glance at your name tag to refresh her memory, she'd (probably) pronounce your name correctly, then give a brief, perhaps somewhat vague description of your business
   c. she'd confidently and energetically share your name, your company name, and a brief one-liner describing the work you do

5. What's your most typical behavior when entering a networking event?
   a. make a beeline for someone you know
   b. seek out a friendly new face and introduce yourself
   c. get something to drink and hope someone friendly will introduce herself

6. How would someone describe your conversational style at networking events?
   a. "Getting her to say anything is like pulling teeth."
   b. "Boy, she's a great listener."
   c. "I couldn't get a word in edgewise."

7. What do you consider an appropriate way to ask for help in making a particular kind of contact?
   a. there *is* no appropriate way to do this
   b. "Who do you know who…?"
   c. "I'm looking for a connection to someone who _____. Do you know anyone like that? Would you be comfortable introducing me to them?"

8. What do you typically want to accomplish at a networking event?
   a. to make one or more contacts for a new potential client or strategic partner *and* to give one or more referrals
   b. to get to the buffet before the food is all gone
   c. to see who you run into

9. When you introduce yourself, what information—other than your name and that of your business—do you share?
   a. your job title
   b. a list of the products and services you offer
   c. a brief statement of the sort of problems you solve for your clients

10. What best describes your attitude toward networking events?
    a. they're okay, especially if food's being served
    b. it's an exciting way to make connections that will benefit others as well as yourself
    c. they're better than a root canal without anesthesia—but not much

These questions address Ten Top Networking Oopses. If you're in the mood for instant gratification, you can jump to appendix A to see how you scored. If you prefer the thrill of discovering and applying new information as you go, read on to find ways to avoid these mistakes and put your best foot forward.

Non-Verbal Communication: Body Language

2

"Actions speak louder than words."
"Walk the talk." "A picture's worth a thousand words."

These and other sayings reflect a crucial networking reality. How we look and behave—in other words, our *body language*—can have more of an impact than what we say and how we say it. A landmark study at the University of Chicago documents this conclusively. Dr. Albert Mehrabian and associates found that **55 percent** of a speaker's impact came from such behaviors as eye contact, posture, stance, and handshake. The key to effective overall communication, then, is to have our non-verbal message enhance our verbal message, rather than contradict it.

This is something of a mixed blessing. The not-so-good news is that even a dynamite introduction of yourself and your services can be greatly undermined by weak body language. The wonderful news is that even a so-so introduction can be made more effective by strong and confident behavior. Following are some potential pitfalls to effective networking and ways to avoid or overcome them.

The Eyes Have It

Chances are that you, like most, have run into people at networking events who seem vitally interested in everything and everyone *but* you. Their eyes flit around the room, look beyond you, or only occasionally connect with you. Such behavior can indicate any number of things. Maybe they're not interested in you, only in themselves. They may be ready to dump you in a heartbeat if they find someone that looks more interesting. Perhaps they're too unsure of themselves to risk making eye contact. Maybe they're just rude. It could even be that their lack of good business etiquette reflects a lack of competency in the way they do business (does the term "shifty-eyed" conjure up any interesting pictures in your mind?).

The other concept to be aware of when it comes to eye contact is *too much of a good thing*. Smart primates know that staring fixedly is a belligerent behavior and often represents a power play. If your listener feels you're trying to one-up her, you'll find it difficult to establish a mutually respectful and beneficial networking relationship.

So, where's the happy medium? Here are some general guidelines to help you establish strong, yet respectful, eye contact.

- ❏ Be especially aware of maintaining eye contact when the other person is speaking; letting your eyes roam at this time is a serious turn-off.
- ❏ Most people are comfortable being on the receiving end of eye contact lasting anywhere from ten to fifteen seconds. After this time, a brief look away—at your hands, around the room, and so on—is appropriate because it ensures the speaker will not feel stared at.
- ❏ When you *do* look away, do so briefly (one to three seconds), then promptly return your gaze to the speaker.

Maintaining appropriate eye contact will go a long way toward helping you establish yourself as considerate, professional, and comfortable to be around. These guidelines are exemplified by one of my fellow Chamber members. When Kathy speaks with me, her warmth and interest are clearly demonstrated by the strong, yet gentle, eye contact she maintains. Her attention and focus make me feel comfortable and important. In turn, I'm eager to help her.

> **Self-Check:**
> 1. Where do your eyes typically spend most of their time? On your networking partner(s)? On the rest of the room? On your shoes? Elsewhere?
> 2. What *specifically* might you do to make your eye contact more effective? Which *one* of these changes will you implement at your next networking event?

Posture

It's also possible to identify two ends of the spectrum when it comes to posture: straight and almost military-like, or slouched. Both of these can give non-verbal messages that hurt your networking. A rigid, overly controlled posture might lead people to think you're humorless and inflexible in your business dealings, while a sloppy, hunched-over posture may imply lack of confidence or sloppiness in business practices. Such conclusions may be totally wrong, but why run the risk of letting a potentially valuable contact draw them? Instead, do yourself a favor. Hold yourself straight and relaxed. You'll look confident, competent, and approachable—real assets at any sort of networking event.

Stance

The way we take up physical space also sends messages, which can be helpful or unhelpful. Different cultures have very different standards for appropriate distances to maintain when speaking with another person. A study of proxemics—interpersonal spatial relationships that reflect a country's culture—indicates that, in the United States, a distance of four to ten feet is suitable for business and social interactions. Anything beyond ten feet is considered public distance, while, going in the opposite direction, a distance of zero to eighteen *inches* is the hallmark of intimate relationships. Friends are welcome within a distance of eighteen inches to four feet. Adhering to these American guidelines helps you match your use of space to the occasion; ignoring them can send a message that's inappropriate for the setting and your purpose in being there.

In the context of networking, your goal is to create a comfortable environment that is conducive to sharing information and resources. The wrong stance can make you look either aggressive or wimpy, neither of which is what you want. A strong stance, however, accomplishes the same goal as does strong posture—it makes you look confident, competent, and approachable.

What's an aggressive stance? One in which your feet are planted wide apart, your elbows are out-thrust, and you invade the other person's space by crowding them. This is very different from a classic wimpy stance in which you try to take up as little room as possible by keeping your feet close together, hands clasped in front of you or stuffed in your pockets, and you appear uncomfortable getting within arm's reach of others.

A confident stance falls nicely between these two extremes, and it starts with a solid base of support: feet approximately shoulder-width apart, weight evenly distributed, knees slightly bent. This helps you both look and feel physically centered. You can test this centering for yourself. Have someone try to push you off-balance when you're standing firm. You'll see that they have to put some real effort into it; your solid base of support allows you to roll with the punches. This is vastly preferable to a closed-in, wimpy stance that will have you looking like a pushover. (Again, have someone try to push you off-balance, then notice how easily they manage it if your feet are too close together.)

Another component of a strong stance is the amount of space you take up. Space equals power in our society. Someone with a large personal space is typically perceived as more powerful than one whose personal space is small. Of course, this can be carried to an obnoxious extreme with an exaggeratedly wide base of support and flailing hand gestures. This is as much to be avoided as the other extreme, in which a tiny personal space says, in effect, "Don't mind me, I don't take up much room." The happy—and effective—medium is to claim enough space so you have room to gesture and move comfortably and still be able to avoid inadvertently bashing your neighbor in the face.

A strong stance has another major benefit to it—not only does it make you *look* confident, it helps you *feel* the same way. What pops into your mind when asked to picture someone who has just won an Olympic gold medal? Chances are you see a person with feet planted strongly and arms reached up in triumph. While you'll want to tone this down for most networking events, you can see how claiming a space sends the message that you're a person who knows what she's doing, is confident in her abilities, and is worth knowing.

> **Self-Check:**
> 1. Look at yourself in a full-length mirror. What sort of posture and stance do you usually maintain? How much space do you take up?
> 2. Is there anything you can do to strengthen the message sent out by your posture and your stance? If so, what *specific* things will you do differently the next chance you get?

Handshake

Your posture and stance send messages even before you make physical contact with another person through a handshake. The handshake is one of the easiest networking behaviors to master, although it's one that's often done poorly.

You've probably dealt with the repulsive dead-fish handshake: limp, no energy, barely any contact between the other person's hand and yours. Though unpleasant, this is at least less painful than the crusher handshake used by people who just don't know their own strength or who are, in some cases, trying to intimidate.

To avoid either mistake, pay attention to that little web of skin between your thumb and forefinger; it makes a handy reference point for a good handshake. Your web and the other person's should come into contact as you firmly grip her hand and give it one or two smooth shakes. (You could say that great handshakers are web masters.)

Another common mistake is to waste time debating over whether or not a handshake is appropriate. Men and women tend to have different reasons for uncertainty in this regard. Men may question whether a woman wants to shake hands, while women may feel it's unnecessary to shake hands with someone they already know. In American business settings, it's a good idea to shake hands with everyone you encounter, whether you know them well or not, to show you're confident and savvy.

NET PROFIT

> **Self-Check:**
> 1. What's your attitude toward shaking hands? How does this affect your physical handshake?
> 2. Think of people who have particularly good handshakes. What do they do that you currently don't? How can you incorporate these effective behaviors into your own handshake?

THE BOTTOM LINE

1. Stay visually and mentally connected with your networking partners by maintaining eye contact, in ten- to fifteen-second chunks, as they speak.
2. Look and feel confident with upright posture and a grounded stance.
3. Develop and use a strong—not crushing—handshake.

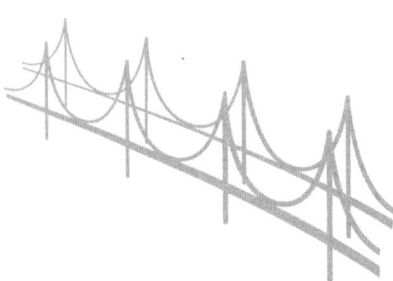

Non-Verbal Communication: Delivery 3

So if body language conveys over half of your message, surely what you *say* makes up the next biggest component, right? Well, actually, no. According to Mehrabian et. al., *how* we say things—our *delivery* of the message—conveys about **38 percent of the meaning**.

When you think of a person who has a great voice, what words come to mind to describe that voice? You might refer to it as rich, smooth, flowing, resonant, pleasantly pitched. Often a person desiring a powerful speaking voice will pay close attention to pitch, volume, inflection, and pace.

Pitch

If you've ever harbored evil thoughts toward a yappy dog because of its shrill, piercing bark, you know that overly high-pitched sounds are irritating. Unfortunately, the same holds true for humans as well as canines. The most eloquent message, delivered in a squeaky high voice, is at real risk for being tuned out, simply because the words are delivered in such an irritating manner. On the flip side, a deep, rumbling bass voice can be hard to understand. Overly high or low pitches can be especially difficult for a hearing-impaired person to handle.

So, how *do* you adjust the treble and bass controls on your voice? The most important thing anyone can do to improve her voice is to breathe properly, which means all the way from your diaphragm. A full breath—one that pushes out your stomach while leaving your shoulders level—is necessary to produce a pleasing tone that makes it easy for your listener to tune into your words. If you think you can't do anything about the pitch of your voice, try this interesting experiment. Standing upright, begin to recite the alphabet or your favorite nursery rhyme, then slowly bend down, continuing to speak, and listen for any difference in the quality of your voice. Many people notice an obvious improvement in the bent-over position because of the support the diaphragm provides to the air moving over their vocal folds (also called vocal cords).

Proper breath, combined with effective projection of air when you speak, will also help eliminate a nasal tone from your voice. An irritating nose voice can seriously detract from the message you're trying to convey, so it's in your best interest to practice projecting your voice from the oral cavity, rather than through the nose. If this is a significant issue for you, spending some time with a professional voice teacher could be a wise investment.

Besides breathing properly, another thing that can help you develop a stronger, more effective voice is simply to be *conscious* of your pitch. If you're used to speaking in a too-high tone of voice, concentrate on speaking lower and slower. If you speak as a bass, remember to lighten up. The goal is to have your pitch, as part of the overall delivery, be unobtrusive, so that it supports—or at least doesn't get in the way of—the verbal message you want to convey.

A pleasing pitch can have even more tangible benefits. My friend Sinden has a wonderfully rich voice, pitched somewhat low for a woman. She's exploring how she can use it to create additional revenue streams by doing commercial voice-overs or reading books onto disc. A strong voice is definitely a multi-faceted asset.

NON-VERBAL COMMUNICATION: DELIVERY

> **Self-Check:**
> 1. Listen to a recording of yourself. Do you cringe at the high-pitched squeak? Are you surprised at the gravelly bass tones? Does it sound like you're talking through your nose? Or are you delighted with the strong, confident voice that's easy to listen to?
> 2. If the pitch of your voice is not attractive to you, what *specific* actions can you take to improve it?

Volume

One episode of the sitcom *Seinfeld* clearly illustrated the potential pitfalls of speaking too softly. Jerry Seinfeld was unable to clearly hear the request of a low talker—a woman whose voice was almost inaudible. Later he found out that he'd inadvertently agreed to help her promote a bug-ugly shirt on national TV.

While you might not face humiliation on such a large scale, you still run the risk of being misunderstood, or even ignored, if the person you're talking to can't hear you easily. Just think back to any networking event you've attended where each person gave a one-minute commercial about her business. Chances are excellent that anyone who didn't crank up the voice volume enough to be heard throughout the room was either ignored or had the value of what she said ignored. Opportunity lost.

On the other hand, no one will appreciate it if, in a networking setting, you belt it out as if you were trying to talk over a rock band. Loud talkers can be viewed as clueless, self-important, or just plain rude. How easy is it to get across an important message if your listener has already discounted what you say because of how you're saying it?

To make it easy for your conversational partner to stay connected with you, focus on speaking loudly enough to be heard over background noise, but no louder. Good breath support from the diaphragm helps you project an appropriate volume at the same time it produces a pleasing, easy-to-listen-to pitch.

> **Self-Check:**
> 1. Do your conversational partners frequently ask you to repeat yourself? Why is that?
> 2. Do you find that your voice is often tired after an event, even if the overall noise level was not that great? What causes that?
> 3. Who can you ask for honest, caring feedback about your speech volume?
> 4. How can you practice improving the volume of your speech?

Inflection

Mismanaging this one non-verbal trait can easily destroy your credibility. Specifically, people who habitually speak with a questioning inflection—raising their voices at the end of sentences and making everything they say sound like a question, rather than a statement—are very often viewed as lacking in confidence and perhaps even competence.

The good news is this counterproductive habit is easily corrected. All that's needed is to be clear about whether you're *asking a question* or *making a statement*, then match the words with the appropriate delivery. A question ends with an upward inflection—you know what I mean? A statement, however, ends with a downward inflection—you know what I mean. Both questions and statements are obviously important parts of conversation. But if you sound like you're asking a question when, in reality, you want to make a statement, you'll weaken your message unnecessarily.

The flip side of a questioning inflection, of course, is making everything you say sound like a pronouncement of unarguable fact. If you appear to rarely ask questions, even in situations where it's called for, you run the risk of appearing inflexible, rigid, and dogmatic—definitely *not* how you want to come across at a networking event where you might meet potential clients or strategic allies. Avoiding this problem is simple: be willing to use the questioning, upward inflection when it's appropriate to seek information, and save the assertive, downward inflection for times when it's appropriate to make a declarative statement.

> **Self-Check:**
> 1. Invest in a micro-recorder and record yourself in a variety of settings. What do you hear in terms of your inflection? Does everything you say sound like a question, even if you're trying to make a declarative statement? Or does everything sound dogmatic, as if you're never willing to ask a question? Or do you have a great, appropriate mix of questioning (upward) inflection and declarative (downward) inflection?
> 2. If you notice you have a habitual upward inflection, practice making your voice go down at the end of all statements.
> 3. If your habitual inflection is downward, practice lightening up and creating an upward inflection any time you ask questions.
> 4. If your inflection typically supports the meaning of your actual words, choose a friend to share your good voice and favorite beverage with, and watch how well the conversation flows.

Pace

The speed at which you speak also has a real impact on how favorably your overall message is received.

The tortoises among us speak very slowly and thoughtfully, and thus avoid bombarding their listeners with a wall of sound. Unfortunately, a listener's brain can process speech much more quickly than your mouth can produce it, which means that someone listening to a tortoise has a *lot* of time for her mind to wander. If someone has tuned out when you're talking, it doesn't really matter how effective your words themselves are, because they're not even making it into the listener's ear.

The hares of the world face a different challenge. They speak so rapidly that they face a number of problems. They create the strong impression that it's all about me-me-me, which is a *major* mistake at networking functions (and in business dealings in general). Their listeners, often unable to get a word in edgewise, may have a great referral to give, but forget about it by the time they have a chance to talk. It's also likely that a hare's victim will try to extricate herself as quickly as possible from the one-sided conversation, in order to seek out someone with whom she can have a true *dialogue*.

So how do you develop a pace that's a happy medium? If you're a tortoise, settle for expressing yourself in an *acceptable* manner, rather than taking a lot of time to find the perfect turn of a phrase. If you're a hare, pause periodically to breathe deeply; this not only keeps your pitch and volume at effective levels, it also gives your listener a chance to take over the conversational reins for a while. Hares will also want to be aware of any tendency to jump into a pause, however slight, in the other person's speech; all this does is encourage the other person to talk faster and faster, in order to get in what she wants to say before being interrupted. Remember, "The opposite of talking isn't listening. The opposite of talking is waiting." (Fran Lebowitz)

Self-Check:
1. Pay attention to upcoming conversations. Do you find yourself interrupting people a lot? Or are you more the one being interrupted? Either situation can indicate some issues with the pace of your speech.
2. Analyze your conversations and determine where you can improve.

THE BOTTOM LINE:
1. Don't yip, don't growl. Develop a speaking voice with an easy-to-listen-to, mid-range pitch, neither too high nor too low.
2. Adjust your personal volume control so there's no need for your listeners to ask you to repeat yourself, nor for them to wear hearing protection in your presence.
3. Say what you mean and mean what you say. Use an upward inflection only when asking a genuine question, and use a strong downward inflection only when making a legitimate statement.
4. Pace yourself. Speak quickly enough to ensure your partner's attention doesn't wander, yet slowly enough that she also has a chance to participate in the conversation.

Verbal Communication

4

Even if you're not a math whiz, it's pretty obvious—with 55 percent of our message being conveyed through our body language and 38 percent through our delivery—that what we say is not nearly important as how we say it and how we behave while speaking. In fact, Mehrabian's research indicates that a measly 7 **percent** of the total message is conveyed through the words we use.

However, the smart networker does not take this as license to be sloppy about her language; on the contrary. Think of the three parts of the message as equivalent to the legs on a stool. This three-way base of support can provide greater strength than any other arrangement *unless* any one component—one leg—is weak. Remember: The goal is to have both non-verbal and verbal components of a message be strong, consistent, and mutually supportive. This is a key tactic used by effective networkers.

Engaging the Listener

We're bombarded by messages all day long and, as a result, most of us have gotten adept at tuning out anything that doesn't immediately grab our attention. The messages that do get past our defenses are those that address a question of vital interest to each of us—"What's in it for me?" (Think of WIIFM as a radio station of infinite variety that *everyone* tunes into.)

How do you take advantage of people's natural self-interest? The best way is to use words to paint a picture and make it easy for your listener to see herself in that picture. Start your work of art by answering the following questions:

- ❑ What kind of *problem* does my product/service solve for my clients?
- ❑ What kind of *pain* does it relieve for them?
- ❑ What do existing clients say they most *appreciate* about my work?
- ❑ I offer _____. *So what?* In other words, how does my product/service *benefit* my clients?
- ❑ What do I *save* for my clients (e.g., time, money, frustration)?
- ❑ How can I help my clients *grow* their businesses?
- ❑ Why is working with me *easy* and *low risk?*

An ideal description of your work is one that uses answers to these questions to tease the listener enough to prompt her to say, "Tell me more," yet provides enough information that she feels you're giving her the straight scoop.

Self-Check:
1. For which of the above questions do you have a brief, powerful answer at the tip of your tongue?
2. If any of the above questions currently lack a good answer, take the time to create and write a powerful response, then practice saying it aloud.
3. Review your answers to the above questions. Revise any that seem to focus on *you* rather than on your *listener* and what she has to gain by knowing you. Practice the new and improved statements until they flow smoothly and engagingly.

Turn-Offs

While some words immediately appeal to a listener, others can lead to a quick disconnect. Since your goal is to share information with your listeners without tripping any of their defenses, steer clear of the following:

- ❏ Talking exclusively about "I–me–mine" instead of focusing on what's important to your listener.
- ❏ Using phrases like "you have to" or "you need to." These directive phrases often bring out the listener's stubborn inner child, who promptly replies, "No, I don't."
- ❏ Saying "you can't." This just begs to be answered by, "Yes, I can."
- ❏ Leading an introduction of yourself with your job title, which makes it very easy for people to tune out if they think they know exactly what it is you do.
- ❏ Being so vague in your description of your work that people get suspicious about what you're *not* telling them.

Self-Check:

1. Listen to yourself. Do the *I*'s, *me*'s, and *mine*'s outnumber the *you*'s and *your*'s? If so, switch the proportions.
2. Think back to the last time you introduced yourself at a networking event. Did your listener understand your description of your work and its benefits? If not, think of the words you used to clarify your meaning, then write out a new introduction that uses more effective phrasing.
3. Once again consider a recent networking event. Does it seem as if people tuned out as soon as they heard what you do? If so, what are some other ways you can describe your work that do *not* start out with your job title? If people stayed tuned in, how did you gain and keep their attention?

The One-Minute Commercial

There are really two types of business people: those who have developed an effective introduction for themselves, and those who haven't. For purposes of effective networking, you want to create a brief and compelling commercial that promotes the value of your work by appealing to the listener's self-interest. By incorporating positive, attractor comments and avoiding negative deflectors, you invite people to learn more about you and, one hopes, enter into a mutually beneficial business relationship as a result.

NET PROFIT

Following are some potential ways to jump-start your commercial. They can lead smoothly into a description of why you're a fabulous resource (see Engaging the Listener earlier in this chapter).

- ❑ "When business owners are struggling with _____, I can help."
- ❑ "I work with business owners who _____."
- ❑ "If you find yourself wondering about _____, I can help you find an answer."
- ❑ "When you've had it up to here with _____, call me."

These and other effective opening comments quickly paint a picture in which the right prospect will instantly see herself. Once her interest is engaged, she'll be curious to learn more about what you do and how you do it. And at that point you've made a solid networking contact.

Self-Check:

1. Review your existing one-minute commercial. See if there are any ways you can spice it up so people are eager to hear more. This may mean telling a mini-story about how you help clients, asking an intriguing question, or describing your work in some unusual way. For example, Amy provides personalized skin care and color consultations. This description is accurate and effective, and it avoids the possible risk of listeners tuning out as they might if she were to introduce herself by saying, "I'm a Mary Kay consultant."

THE BOTTOM LINE:

1. Polish and refine your one-minute commercial until it has a great balance between providing too much information and not enough.
2. Take advantage of low-risk situations (e.g., educational seminars on networking offered by Chambers of Commerce or other business organizations) to practice your commercial until it's polished and engaging. Remember, practice makes perfect.

Deciding Where to Invest Your Time, Money, and Energy

5

There are a host of organizations and events out there, all begging for your involvement. Since time is a precious and limited commodity for the typical business owner, the smart networker will involve herself in only those activities that are likely to give the highest return on time, money, and energy invested. Whichever organizations and events you choose, you'll maximize your results by remembering two key principles: Net*work* is a verb, and what goes around comes around.

It's unrealistic to think that simply joining an organization and attending events now and again will automatically cause business to flow to you. It's up to you, as a savvy networker, to attend events and meetings regularly, contribute ideas as well as time, and be on the lookout for ways you can be of service to others. All too often, someone will either attend events sporadically or flit from one group to another, trying to make that big score, then disappear. Ivan Misner, founder of Business Network International (BNI), refers to this practice as "scorched-earth networking."

So, what are some selection criteria you can use to evaluate the different organizations that would be delighted to take your money? Clear answers to the following questions provide good guidance by showing you whether an organization's membership matches your needs. Organizational staff or elected officers can answer some of the questions for you; other questions require you to attend some events and draw your own conclusions. See appendix B for a version of the following questions in a form you can photocopy to keep track of the different organizations you evaluate.

- ❏ What types of people typically join this organization?
- ❏ What sort of contacts am I looking to make? Prospective new clients? Referral sources? Potential strategic partners?
- ❏ If I operate multiple businesses or have a multi-faceted primary business, on which specific venture will I focus this networking?
- ❏ For B2B, or *business-to-business* service providers: Am I looking for small-business owners or executives in larger corporations? What size company is an ideal prospect for me in terms of revenues, number of employees, or other useful criteria? Am I looking to connect with start-up, young, or established businesses?
- ❏ For B2C, or *business-to-consumer* service providers: What are the demographics and/or psychographics of my ideal prospect? (*Note:* "Everyone" is not a useful way to describe your target market!)
- ❏ Is there a match between the existing membership and the types of contacts I'm seeking?
- ❏ Does the membership include people who also serve my target market, although in some complementary field? (For example, a business attorney might seek contact with CPA's because they both specialize in small-to-medium businesses; their services are related, not competitive.)
- ❏ Is the primary purpose of the group to provide community service? Networking for business-building purposes? Support for a particular cause? Something else?
- ❏ Which of these goals is most in line with what I want to get out of my membership?
- ❏ What specific opportunities exist for becoming active in the organization? Ongoing events? Committees? Leadership roles?
- ❏ How much does it cost to join and participate? Annual dues? Program fees? Other costs?
- ❏ How much time and money am I willing to invest in networking in this organization?

- ❑ Would I feel good about being associated with these people and this group? Is the chemistry good?
- ❑ What do existing members have to say about the organization? How long have they been members? How has the group met their needs? What do they consider the three greatest benefits about their membership? What activities have they found to be most valuable to them, and why? What group activities/procedures would they change if they could?
- ❑ On a scale of 1 to 10, with 1 being totally not worthwhile and 10 being this is a perfect fit for me, how does this organization rate?

Ideally, you'll be able to evaluate the appropriateness of an organization before actually joining it. In reality, though, you may find a group that sounded like it would be valuable turns out to be less so once you're actively involved in it. Richard, a marketing consultant, illustrates how to deal with this situation. He actively participates in any organization he joins. If, after a year or so, he finds it's not paying off for him, he drops membership in that underperforming group and devotes more time and energy to the groups that *are* resulting in valuable contacts for him.

Self-Check:

1. How do various organizations compare, based on answers to the above questions?
2. Based on this comparison, which organizations give you the best value for your investment of time and money?

THE BOTTOM LINE:

1. Be systematic and consistent in evaluating the potential value of various organizations.
2. Be realistic in deciding your budgets of time and money.
3. Commit to being an active, involved member in all organizations you join.

Preparing for the Event

6

You've decided what organizations to join, and you're getting ready to attend your first networking event as a new member. You've strengthened your non-verbals, polished your verbals, and are raring to go. What more can you do to ensure the event is profitable and enjoyable, rather than merely okay? Use the following checklist to ensure that you're prepared to be—and do—your best.

- ❑ Take more business cards than you think you'll use; getting caught without cards at a networking event is a mondo no-no. Stock your favorite card-holder and stash it in the pocket most convenient to your dominant hand. Then make sure you have multiple back-ups—in your wallet, briefcase, planner (if you use a non-electronic one), glove compartment of your car.

- ❑ Carry your cards in a good quality holder. Yes, it's cheap to use the flimsy plastic ones that are so common, but do you really want your business tools to scream "Cheap"? Instead, invest a few dollars in a holder made of leather or—my personal favorite—wood. I like the latter because it's unusual, is a good conversation starter, and is one more way I can stand out from the crowd.

- ❑ Be sure you've designated a separate location (pocket, planner, etc.) for cards you collect. (It *really* doesn't look good if you give a hot new prospect someone else's card by mistake.)

NET PROFIT

- ❏ If you choose to take any hard copy marketing materials with you, be sure all the copies you have are clean, uncreased, and easily accessible.
- ❏ Have a functional pen handy for making notes on business cards you collect. It's especially crucial to have a reminder of something you've promised to do for your new acquaintance. (Be aware that while the practice of writing on someone's card is typically acceptable in America, people in other cultures, e.g., China, may consider it very offensive.)
- ❏ Make sure you have sticky notes or a small notepad for any "to do" items that might crop up.
- ❏ Identify in advance a variety of complaints or comments that indicate a need for your service; listen for these so you can quickly identify prospects.
- ❏ Create a wish list of the people you'd like to connect with. This list may include specific individuals, representatives of a particular company, business owners in a particular industry or geographic area, or any other people who come under the heading "good folks to know."
- ❏ Practice your one-minute commercial *out loud* to be sure it flows off your tongue as smoothly as it reads on paper.
- ❏ Confirm that you know the location of the event and how to get there. Get directions from the event organizers or an Internet site if you're not positive you know where you're going. (Why risk feeling frazzled because of a late arrival?)
- ❏ Allow extra time to get to the venue, taking into account probable traffic levels as well as any stops you might make on the way. This has myriad benefits (see chapter 7, Behavior at the Event).

Self-Check:
1. Which steps in the above checklist do you already do well?
2. Which ones have you done only so-so in the past? Address these explicitly before the next event you attend.
3. What shape is your business card holder in? If it looks like it has a lot of miles on it, when will you replace it? What will you replace it with?
4. Check your back-up sources for business cards. If they aren't fully stocked, take care of that now.
5. Consider putting together a travel pack of items you'll need at any networking event: business cards, notepad/sticky notes, pen, marketing materials, written list of individuals or companies you want to connect with.

THE BOTTOM LINE:
1. Treat planning and preparation like the crucial steps they are. "If you fail to plan, you're planning to fail" has become a cliché simply because of its fundamental truth.
2. Resist the temptation to assume you have everything you need for an event. Take a few moments to physically verify you have directions, your travel pack, and anything else you might need.

Behavior at the Event

7

It's moment-of-truth time. Now you get to benefit from all your pre-event planning and preparation. Be sure your behavior at a networking event portrays you as a savvy businessperson who has a lot to offer others. Here are a number of ways to make you stand out from the crowd.

Managing Time

One of the most versatile networking strategies you can apply is to arrive early at an event. This stacks the deck in your favor in numerous ways.

- ❑ You'll be calm and collected, as opposed to frazzled because of leaving the office late, getting stuck in traffic, and so forth.
- ❑ You'll have time to give your appearance a final check to ensure your hair is neat, you've gotten rid of all the dog hair on your jacket, you don't have any broccoli in your teeth...
- ❑ If the sponsoring organization has printed name tags for attendees, you can look over all of them. This allows you to identify interesting potential contacts by corporate or individual name and then to be on the lookout for them when they arrive.
- ❑ At events where you'll be seated for a meal or presentation, you'll have your choice of seats facing the podium. This allows you to see a speaker without turning your head or shifting your chair.

- ❑ You'll also be able to stake a claim on a seat near one end of the room, rather than right in the middle. This way, when it's time for you to stand and give your one-minute commercial (a very common practice at networking events), you can face the entire room. You won't have your back to anyone or need to turn back and forth like an oscillating sprinkler in an attempt to make eye contact with people behind you. (See the next section, Managing Logistics, for ideas on how to avoid a common seating faux pas.)

- ❑ As one of the first arrivals, you'll be in a natural position to act like a host by welcoming people who arrive after you. This will make you a hero to those attendees who may otherwise be reluctant to take the initiative by introducing themselves to someone new. Also, it will allow you to create a hub of energy and activity that will draw others to it as they enter—an easy and effective way to attract potential valuable contacts to yourself and others.

A common format at networking events is a conversational free-for-all followed by a go-around, in which everyone in the room has a chance to present her one-minute commercial to everyone else. This gives you a great chance to share an intriguing snapshot of your business with potentially dozens of people. In the interest of saving time, attendees at a large gathering will sometimes be asked to limit their commercials to just their name and that of their business (the networking equivalent of name, rank, and serial number). You can sneak in more information while still being pretty compliant by adding a tag line (of no more than a dozen or so words) to your name. For example, Ken offers custom men's clothing and does talks on business etiquette. His cheater commercial sounds like this: "Morgan's Custom Clothiers—your 2nd chance to make a 1st impression." This technique allows you to be respectful of others while making effective use of your moment in the sun.

Even when you're *not* asked to keep your commercial very brief, it's still in your own best interest to apply the KISS principle—Keep It Short and Simple. If your one-minute commercial drags into nearly five minutes (which happens surprisingly often), you'll lose your audience's attention. This means you've also lost your chance to interest them in learning more about you and, one hopes, spending money on your fabulous product or service.

> **Self-Check:**
> 1. When do you typically arrive at networking events? If you tend to be a late arrival, what specifically can you do to change this unproductive behavior?
> 2. Do you have your cheater tag line ready for those occasions when you're asked to only give your name and company name? If not, take time to develop it now, remembering to keep it short and simple.
> 3. Do you know how long your one-minute commercial *really* lasts? If it's done in sixty seconds—yay for you. If not, write out and practice aloud a more concise version.

Managing Logistics

Some people fail to take full advantage of go-arounds, either because of an ineffective verbal message or a distracting non-verbal one. While your pre-event prep will have taken care of the former, the latter must be addressed on the spot.

If everyone is standing around in a circle, step forward slightly when it's your turn to speak, then step back when you're done. If you're seated, wait until you've stood up straight and tall before starting to speak, and *quit* speaking before you sit down (the talking-while-sitting-down maneuver is awkward and unprofessional). These are two of the easiest ways to convey a strong message.

Speaking of seating arrangements, how often have you attended an event where co-workers sat right next to each other? How often have you done this yourself? While it's a wonderful perk to enjoy your colleagues' company, a networking event is *not* the place for it. The whole point of such an event is to connect to *new* people with whom you might develop a mutually beneficial relationship. Sitting with colleagues—no matter how fun or comfortable it may be—wastes opportunity, time, and money.

However, there *is* a simple way to combine ease and effectiveness. Sit at the same table as your co-worker, if you like; just make sure that each of you is sitting next to two people (one on either side) who are new acquaintances. This is a terrific arrangement: there's still some ease and comfort, because you can easily look up and catch your colleague's eyes, but you have far more opportunity to talk to someone new about your business.

If you've done a good job with your one-minute commercial and your mealtime conversations, chances are excellent that people will either seek you out to learn more about what you do or will want to introduce you to someone they know who could use your services. Having someone approach you is a golden opportunity for you to easily establish yourself as someone in the know about networking. How? By placing your name tag on your *right* shoulder. Why? The theory is this: Since people typically shake with their right hands, they're already angled toward the right side of the person they're greeting. Having your name tag on that side allows the other person to easily read your name. Simple and effective.

If you're networking effectively, you'll have quite a few cards after an event. How do you keep straight what you discussed with whom, and—especially important—how do you ensure that you'll remember to follow through on any promised activities? An easy way to do this is to take notes on the back of the card, after asking the person if it's acceptable to her that you do so. While most Americans will readily assent, many businesspeople from other cultures would find it extremely rude for you to deface the card, so be aware of these cultural differences. (See chapter 8, Effective Follow-Up, for ways to join the minority of businesspeople who actually *do what they say they're going to do.*)

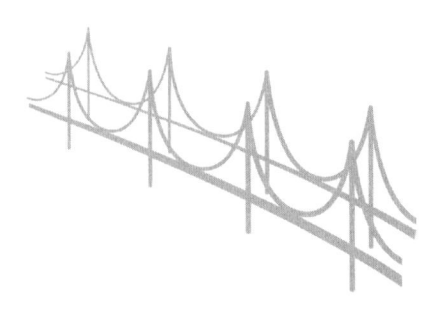

BEHAVIOR AT THE EVENT

Self-Check:
1. How do you manage your personal space when doing go-arounds at a networking event? Do you step forward or stand up so as to be noticed when you speak? If not, how can you remember to do so next time?
2. With whom do you sit? If you realize you and your co-workers seem to be joined at the hip when at networking events, figure out ways to create a security blankie for yourself while still making new contacts.
3. Where do you wear your name tag? (Right handers, pay special attention to this: it's really easy for us to use our dominant hand to slap the tag on the left shoulder.)
4. What's your strategy for keeping track of what you discussed with whom? How can you make this strategy more effective?

Managing Personal Interactions

You may be wondering, "But what if I don't know how to get these great conversations started? I'm lousy at small talk! Mayday!" Good news. You can give your confidence and comfort a great boost by creating a road map for an interesting dialogue, using the conversational stack taught by Dale Carnegie Training.

As you read through the following list, take a few seconds to picture each item as it's added:

- ❑ Imagine an enormous name plate, such as you'd find on someone's desk.
- ❑ Balanced on top of this is a house.
- ❑ Perched on the house's chimney is a work glove.
- ❑ This glove is reaching into the sky and grabbing a small airplane.
- ❑ Where the propellers normally would be, you see, instead, a tennis racquet and a baseball bat.
- ❑ Inside the cockpit there is a bright flashing light.

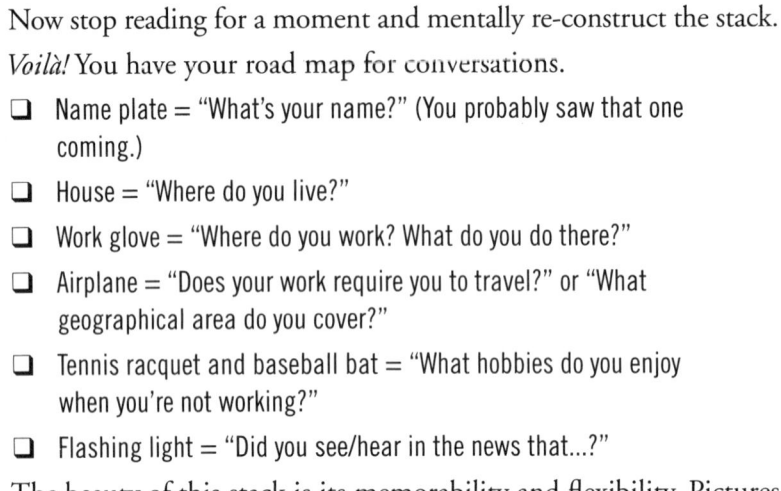

Now stop reading for a moment and mentally re-construct the stack. *Voilà!* You have your road map for conversations.

- ❏ Name plate = "What's your name?" (You probably saw that one coming.)
- ❏ House = "Where do you live?"
- ❏ Work glove = "Where do you work? What do you do there?"
- ❏ Airplane = "Does your work require you to travel?" or "What geographical area do you cover?"
- ❏ Tennis racquet and baseball bat = "What hobbies do you enjoy when you're not working?"
- ❏ Flashing light = "Did you see/hear in the news that...?"

The beauty of this stack is its memorability and flexibility. Pictures are typically easy to recall (remember how you crafted your one-minute commercial to *paint a picture* in which your listener can see herself). And since you'll be able to readily picture the completed stack, you'll be able to easily pick and choose topics and the order in which you want to introduce them. For example, if you don't feel like asking where your conversational partner lives, you can skip the house and go straight to asking where she works.

Some people feel that, no matter what the conversational topic, a high-energy, gregarious style is required to be an effective networker. While this can be useful, it's certainly not a requirement. In fact, a high-energy person who loves to talk may actually face a greater challenge than a quieter person. A good networker remembers that the person she's talking to wants to know, "What's in it for me?" How can you answer that question if *you're* talking so much you don't give the other person a chance to share what's important to her? Leading with your true style—whether low-key or turbo-charged—is a mark of authenticity and is key to effective networking. You'll have greater success and find networking more enjoyable if you adapt new skills, new tools, to your own style.

Whether outgoing or reserved, people are likely to run into situations where they feel ready to move on but don't know how to extricate themselves from their current conversation. An excellent strategy is to prepare, in advance, a number of verbal pry bars you can use as needed. Following are some samples. Again, take what you feel is useful and change the wording if you want so it's easy and comfortable for you to say.

- ❑ "I promised myself I'd meet as many interesting people at this event as I could, and you've gotten me off to a great start. Thanks! Now I'm going to go see what other neat types I can connect with."
- ❑ "I'd really like to talk with you longer in a quieter setting. How do you feel about getting together over coffee to continue this discussion? Do you have your planner with you?"
- ❑ "I know we're both looking to make as many good initial contacts as possible today. What do you say to wrapping up our conversation for now so we can both track down additional interesting folks?"
- ❑ "I've been keeping my eye open tonight for a supplier/vendor/colleague I want to talk to, and I've just spotted her. Will you excuse me so I can go connect with her? Thanks!"
- ❑ "I don't want to monopolize your time, because I know we're both here to make a number of good contacts. Shall we see what other people are here?"

Keep in mind that you're probably doing yourself *and* your conversational partner a favor by enabling each of you to connect with more people.

Self-Check:

1. Do you have a clear mental checklist of conversational topics you can introduce? If not, take time to develop one and commit it to memory.
2. Do you keep the focus on the other person when in conversation? Remember, she's wanting to know "*What's in it for me* if I talk with you?"
3. Do you have some exit strategies prepared to help you move on from a conversation that's run its course? If not, take time to come up with some and practice them out loud so that they'll flow easily when you need them.

THE BOTTOM LINE:

1. Create a successful networking event by being prepared, confident, and intent on helping others, and by expecting success (because we tend to find what we're looking for).
2. When presenting your one-minute commercial, follow that time-honored advice: "Stand up, speak up, shut up."

Effective Follow-Up

8

For many people, the most challenging part of networking occurs *after* the event concludes. Of all the activities that make up networking, the *follow-up* has some of the greatest potential to make or break your overall success. Unfortunately, for many of us this is a business skill that falls far short of our performance in other areas of work.

There are any number of reasons for poor follow-up. You may not know exactly how to respond to a request for information, or, even if you do, you may not *want* to respond. You may feel you have no time. Perhaps your backlog of stuff to follow up with is so overwhelming that you want to (and do?) bury your head in the sand, even though you know that maintenance of any activity is far easier than damage control.

As you've probably experienced at one time or another, there are numerous problems with any of these approaches. Puzzling or distasteful tasks only get worse if you delay them; in addition, it feels like an albatross on steroids is hanging around your shoulders. Waiting until you have enough time is the same thing as putting off a task indefinitely. And doing nothing at all not only fails to move you forward, but can actually set you back by sending a message that you can't be trusted to do what you say you'll do.

The thing about follow-up is that it's a high-impact activity that often has no formal deadline associated with it. This is a prime example of the difference between importance and urgency. Consider the following grid:

	Not Important	Important
Urgent	I: time wasters	II: fires
Not Urgent	III: busy work	IV: opportunities

The first quadrant, *not important but urgent*, includes time wasters such as interruptions, most ringing phones, and many meetings. There's some in-your-face quality to these activities that demands you handle them *now*, but, in the long run, they typically don't have a significant impact on your bottom line one way or the other.

The second quadrant of *important and urgent* activities are fires that have some deadline associated with them, as well as serious consequences if they're not handled (think of how quickly you jump to fix a problem with your biggest client).

The third quadrant of *neither urgent nor important* activities is made up of busy work (ever find yourself re-arranging your desktop in order to avoid some other task?).

Many items requiring follow-up are *opportunities*, which fall into the fourth quadrant, *important but not urgent*. Such activities can have a significant positive impact on your business, but they lack a clear deadline. This can be a real problem because, while failing to follow up may not create an obvious crisis, it definitely can result in losing a chance to substantially improve your business. If you've told a contact you'll send information to her, you must *do what you say you'll do*. Many people are so poor at follow-up that simply sending any information you promised can immediately put you in a noteworthy minority.

The question is, How can you take advantage of all the opportunities represented by the networking contacts you've made? The single most important thing you can do is create a *system* that makes following up simple and relatively painless. There are any number of systems that will get the job done; the trick is to find one that works *for you*. Irene, a

EFFECTIVE FOLLOW-UP

personal and professional life coach, has found Outlook Express to be useful for managing her contacts. Even though a number of people have encouraged her to use software like ACT! or Goldmine instead, she sticks with what's comfortable for her. The result: She uses her system consistently, which results in exceptional follow-up.

Following are some suggested ways for managing follow-up. Select and blend these activities—and feel free to add others of your own choosing—to develop a system that will put you in the elite category of contacts who follow up promptly.

- ❏ When scheduling a networking event, don't just put the event proper into your planner: *Schedule time for follow-up* to be done as soon as possible after the event itself. Ideally, you'll follow up within forty-eight hours of the event, at the latest.

- ❏ Note on every newly acquired business card the date and name of the event where you made the contact, assuming you haven't already taken care of this while at the event.

- ❏ Enter each name into your contact management software and/or e-mail address book. Investing in a business card scanner will go a *long* way toward making this task less onerous. (See appendix D.)

- ❏ If you have a major backlog of business cards you've collected but not organized, here's a great tip: Each morning and each afternoon set a kitchen timer for nine minutes; organize/enter contact information into the appropriate software during that time, then let that task go. You can tolerate almost anything for just nine minutes, and you'll have the satisfaction of knowing you're taking charge and making progress. (Feng Shui experts will tell you that nine is an auspicious number *and* that de-cluttering your work space allows energy—which can come in the form of money—to flow more freely and easily. See how true this holds for you.)

- ❏ Follow the advice of Jedi Master Yoda: "Do or do not. There is no 'try'." In other words, either commit to follow up or commit not to; just don't kid yourself that you'll try to get to it. If you had a brain burp and promised to follow up with a contact you *know* is not a viable one for you, simply admit it quickly and—just as quickly—respond to the person anyway. Explain that, after further consideration, you've concluded your product or service really isn't a good fit for her business. Thank her for her interest and wish her success in meeting her business goals. Try to provide her with *some* type of assistance—a referral to another service provider, a copy of a relevant article, a contact at a leads-passing group, or whatever. You'll make a good impression despite having extricated yourself from an unworkable situation.

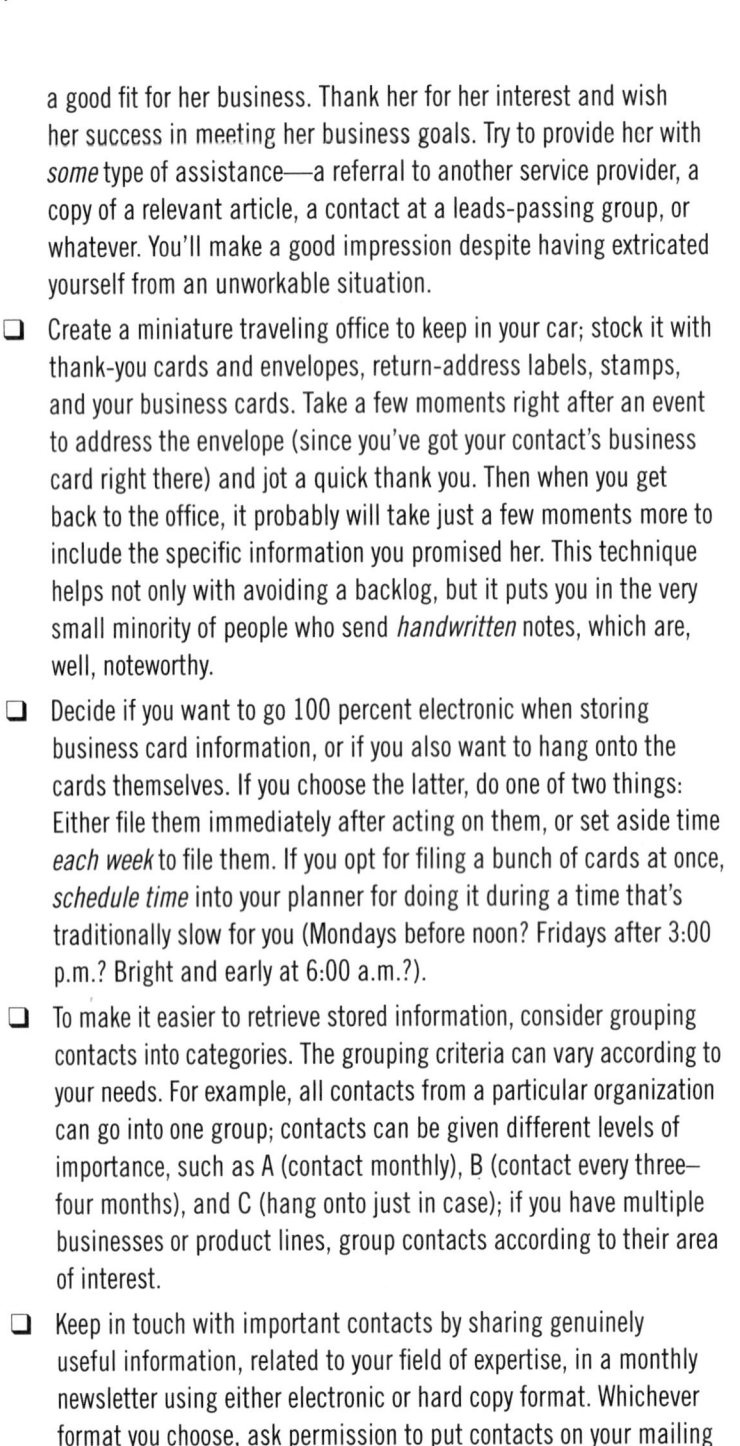

- ❑ Create a miniature traveling office to keep in your car; stock it with thank-you cards and envelopes, return-address labels, stamps, and your business cards. Take a few moments right after an event to address the envelope (since you've got your contact's business card right there) and jot a quick thank you. Then when you get back to the office, it probably will take just a few moments more to include the specific information you promised her. This technique helps not only with avoiding a backlog, but it puts you in the very small minority of people who send *handwritten* notes, which are, well, noteworthy.

- ❑ Decide if you want to go 100 percent electronic when storing business card information, or if you also want to hang onto the cards themselves. If you choose the latter, do one of two things: Either file them immediately after acting on them, or set aside time *each week* to file them. If you opt for filing a bunch of cards at once, *schedule time* into your planner for doing it during a time that's traditionally slow for you (Mondays before noon? Fridays after 3:00 p.m.? Bright and early at 6:00 a.m.?).

- ❑ To make it easier to retrieve stored information, consider grouping contacts into categories. The grouping criteria can vary according to your needs. For example, all contacts from a particular organization can go into one group; contacts can be given different levels of importance, such as A (contact monthly), B (contact every three–four months), and C (hang onto just in case); if you have multiple businesses or product lines, group contacts according to their area of interest.

- ❑ Keep in touch with important contacts by sharing genuinely useful information, related to your field of expertise, in a monthly newsletter using either electronic or hard copy format. Whichever format you choose, ask permission to put contacts on your mailing list and keep the shamelessly overt commercials to a minimum. This same strategy can be applied to web logs ("blogs").

Self-Check:
1. What's your current method of follow up? If you were to rate it on a scale of 1 ("*What* follow-up?") to 5 (flawless follow-up), how would it score?
2. If there's room for improvement, which of the techniques discussed in this chapter will you implement? *When* will you commit to making these changes? Have you scheduled the time in your planner yet?

THE BOTTOM LINE:

1. Invest whatever time and effort is necessary to develop a plan for follow up that you can implement and maintain. The rewards will be huge.
2. Whether you're in damage control mode or maintenance mode, follow Nike's advice and *"just do it."*

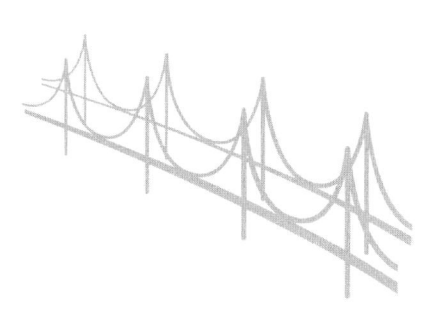

Networking for New College Graduates

9

Some college graduates are already working in jobs that relate to their field of study. These folks certainly have a leg up on using networking contacts to find a permanent and, one hopes, even better job after graduation.

However, if you're searching for that *first* job in your field, there are still a number of ways to use effective networking to expedite the process. (Note: If your college days are long gone, just bookmark this chapter for your son or daughter.)

Commercials for Grads

First of all, remember that a recent college grad is in just as much need of an effective one-minute commercial as anyone else. Prospective employers are definitely asking themselves, "*What's in it for me* if I hire this person?" Your job is to make it as easy as possible for them to see you as an outstanding member of their team.

The same principles that a business owner uses to develop a commercial for her business can be used, with modifications, to develop a great commercial for you when you graduate. Answers to the following questions will give you the raw material you need to build it:

- ❏ What kind of *problems* have I demonstrably solved in my course work, as well as in any jobs I've had?
- ❏ What kind of *pain* could an employer avoid by hiring me instead of someone else for this position?

NET PROFIT

- ❏ What have professors, fellow students, and employers *appreciated* most about my work to date?
- ❏ I studied and got good grades in _____. *So what?* In other words, how will my educational and work experience *benefit* my new employer?
- ❏ What can I *save* for my employer (e.g., if you're a genuinely fast learner, you'll save training time and costs for her)?
- ❏ How can I help my employer *grow* her business/improve her bottom line?
- ❏ Why is hiring me and working with me *easy* and *low risk?*

> **Self-Check:**
> 1. Do you know how to answer the above questions? If not, take the time to write out and orally practice the answers so they'll flow smoothly during interviews.
> 2. How can you incorporate these answers into the appropriate sections of your resume (e.g., Objective, Summary of Qualifications, Accomplishments)?

Venues for Networking

Once you've developed and refined your commercial, you're ready to use it in as many appropriate situations as you can find. Consider the following places where you can grab a potential employer's attention with a compelling description of why they'd be lucky to have you join their company.

- ❏ Your college's or university's placement office is an obvious place to hook up with your target market.
- ❏ Check with local Chambers of Commerce to see if they have a section on their websites where you can post a resume (which is, essentially, your written commercial).
- ❏ And speaking of written promotion, although searching the classified section is the exact opposite of networking as a job-finding strategy, it *is* another avenue to use. Responding to ads gives you the opportunity to share, through your resume and cover letter, some of the dynamic answers you've developed to

NETWORKING FOR NEW COLLEGE GRADUATES

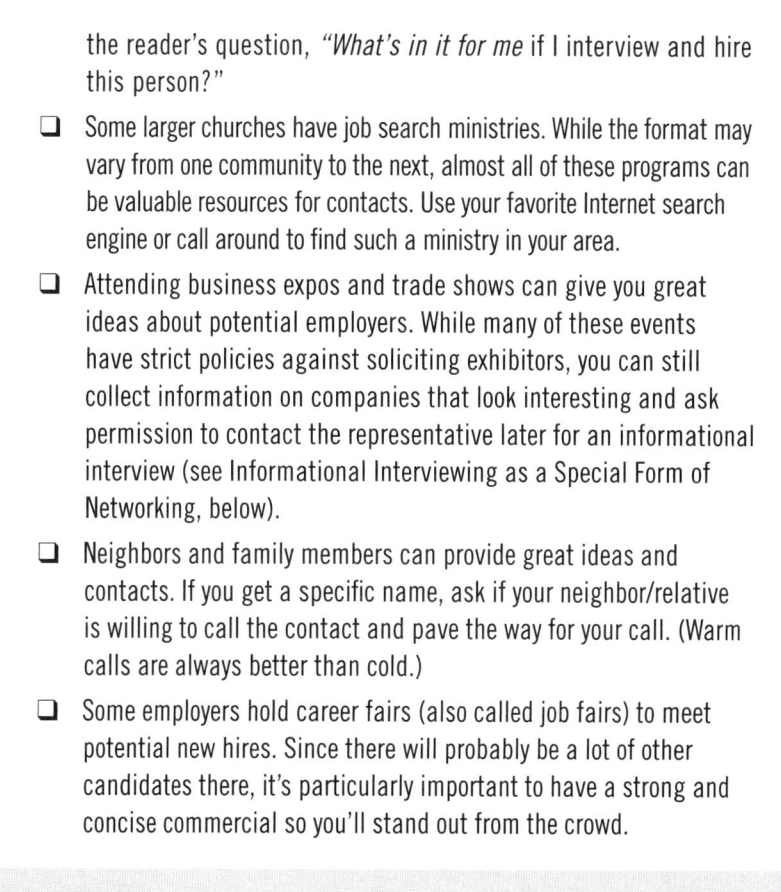

the reader's question, *"What's in it for me* if I interview and hire this person?"

❑ Some larger churches have job search ministries. While the format may vary from one community to the next, almost all of these programs can be valuable resources for contacts. Use your favorite Internet search engine or call around to find such a ministry in your area.

❑ Attending business expos and trade shows can give you great ideas about potential employers. While many of these events have strict policies against soliciting exhibitors, you can still collect information on companies that look interesting and ask permission to contact the representative later for an informational interview (see Informational Interviewing as a Special Form of Networking, below).

❑ Neighbors and family members can provide great ideas and contacts. If you get a specific name, ask if your neighbor/relative is willing to call the contact and pave the way for your call. (Warm calls are always better than cold.)

❑ Some employers hold career fairs (also called job fairs) to meet potential new hires. Since there will probably be a lot of other candidates there, it's particularly important to have a strong and concise commercial so you'll stand out from the crowd.

Self-Check:
1. What networking opportunities have you identified as part of your overall job-search strategy? Why did you select the ones you did?
2. How many different techniques are you using to get in front of prospective employers? Resist the temptation to put all of your eggs in any one basket.

Informational Interviewing as a Special Form of Networking

As a job seeker, the term *interview* probably conjures an image of you and a recruiter discussing a specific job opening at her company. However, another type of interview can be just as important to your ultimate success. The last thing you want to do is spend time and energy getting into a particular industry or company, only to discover that it's a poor

45

fit for you. Informational interviewing is an excellent way to research a company or industry before accepting a job offer. It provides a chance to become an informed consumer and to apply your networking skills.

The first and most crucial thing to remember about informational interviewing is that it truly is a means of gathering information, *not* a way to con the person into interviewing you for a job. If your professionalism leads the interviewee to suggest you apply for a position, fantastic, but getting a job offer is not the primary goal of an informational interview. If you show your integrity by focusing on gathering information and being respectful of your interviewee's time, you'll make an excellent impression and may very well be added to her future file of potential candidates for positions that open up later.

The first question is, "Who do I interview?" There are a number of ways of identifying people who can be founts of information for you:

- ❏ Find out who, among your family, friends, and neighbors, are happy with their current employers. Ask if they can recommend someone at the company for you to meet with and if they'll share their own experiences.
- ❏ See if any local companies are mentioned in lists or articles about the best companies to work for. If so, ask people you know if *they* know anyone at those companies, and see if you can get a verbal introduction to that person.
- ❏ Read the local papers, especially the business sections, to identify people who sound interesting or who work for interesting companies.
- ❏ If you're researching a particular industry, check the resource section of the library to see if there's a local chapter of that industry's professional association. If so, interview the chapter's officers.
- ❏ Consider interviewing people at companies with a history of corporate philanthropy. There's a good chance that a company concerned about what happens beyond its four walls will also take care of its employees (that could be you).
- ❏ Decide if you prefer a small, medium, or large company and focus on people at that size of organization. If you're not sure, interview people at all three.

Ideally, a friend or acquaintance will be able to introduce you to someone who would be a good information source for you. Unfortunately, this won't always be possible, in which case you get to expand your comfort zone by contacting a total stranger.

Opinions vary as to whether it's best to make your initial contact by phone, e-mail, or regular mail. Each method has its advantages and disadvantages, so the choice may well come down to deciding which one is most comfortable for you and at which you're most adept. Regardless of your choice, remember the following points:

- *Any* time you call—and actually connect with—someone on the phone, give your name and immediately ask something along the lines of, "Have I caught you at a time when you have a minute for a quick question?"
- If she indicates you've caught her at a bad time, ask what other time would be better.
- If she says she has that minute, explain that you would like to do an informational interview with her, that you *guarantee* to take no more than thirty minutes of her time, and that you're available at her convenience; then ask if she's willing to help you out. When she says yes, make the appointment, confirm location, and thank her in advance for her help.
- If making the initial contact by e-mail, remember two things: Most people have spam filters, and, even if they don't, you still have to get through their own *mental* filters. Thus, be direct and honest when filling in the subject line. "Can you help me by granting me an *informational* interview?" is attention getting, straightforward, and subtly flattering, and appeals to the person's desire to help.
- If your initial contact is by regular mail, keep the letter short and to the point. Let your prospect know you'll soon be calling her to arrange a time convenient for her.

Keep in mind that the people you're likely to want to interview are busy and will expect you to keep your word about taking up a limited amount of their time. Based on personal experience, however, I recommend you be aware it might be harder to stick to your timetable than you expect. People love to talk about themselves, and it might be a challenge to rein in your interviewee. For this reason, you might want to ask your most important questions first. As you approach the end of the agreed-upon time, comment that you have just another quick question or two before you run out of time. If the interviewee is having such a good time that she wants to give you more time, go for it. Thank her, ask when she will have to wrap up *really*, then forge ahead.

So, you might be wondering, what is this person going to so enjoy talking about? Answer: the most fascinating subject in the world (i.e., herself). By the same token, you, as the interviewer, want your time to be well spent, so you want to ask questions that will be most useful in making a decision about whether or not to pursue a particular type of work. Consider the following:

- ❏ What prompted you to go into this field in the first place?
- ❏ How does the reality stack up to your initial expectations?
- ❏ Which aspects of the job do you enjoy most? For what reasons?
- ❏ Which aspects are most challenging? For what reasons?
- ❏ How long have you been in this position? This industry?
- ❏ Is there anything you would have done differently to prepare yourself even better for success in this field?
- ❏ What skills are most important to you in your position?
- ❏ If I were to pursue work in this field, is there any type of additional training or experience you recommend I get?
- ❏ Are there any other people in this field that would be useful for me to meet with? Would you be willing to call them and let them know I'll be contacting them soon?

Once the interview is completed, send out a *handwritten* thank you note *that same day*. Not only does this get a task off your "to do" list, it also distinguishes you as someone with good manners, business acumen, and timely follow-up—all of which will be attractive to someone who just might be in a position to hire you when a position opens at her company.

Self-Check:
1. Do you have your one-minute commercial prepared and polished? If not, take time to develop one now and practice until you can deliver it smoothly and effectively.
2. What questions do you want to ask the people with whom you conduct informational interviews?
3. What are your highest priority questions?
4. Do you have a supply of professional looking thank you notes ready for use?

THE BOTTOM LINE:
1. An accurate and enticing one-minute commercial is an essential tool for the college graduate.
2. The more networking you do, using this commercial, the more quickly you're likely to land a dynamite job.
3. Use both job interviews and informational interviews as ways to increase your business contacts and further hone your networking skills.

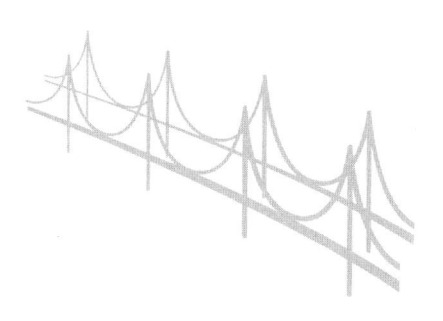

Networking in Your Current Industry 10

Say you're established in a position you enjoy. How do you apply your networking skills to advance your career? There are any number of situations you can use to increase your visibility and credibility. See how many of the following you're currently taking advantage of:

- ❏ Join and actively participate in industry-specific professional associations.

- ❏ Become active on committees, whether in professional associations or at work. Better yet, seek out leadership roles in these committees.

- ❏ With your manager's permission, volunteer for high-profile tasks within your company, even if they don't directly relate to your day-to-day work (e.g., chairing a United Way campaign, organizing a blood drive, and so forth).

- ❏ Take continuing education/college courses to improve your industry-related skills as well as general business knowledge. Make it a point to connect with both fellow learners and instructors.

- ❏ Alternatively, see what the requirements are for *teaching* at a local college as adjunct faculty. See if there are ways to connect with other faculty (e.g., at meetings, by team teaching a class or course) and, of course, be readily available and helpful to the

NET PROFIT

learners in your class. Anyone who is engaged in either teaching or learning in her field of interest is a good potential networking contact for you.

- ❏ Become actively involved with a local service organization (e.g., Lions, Rotary, Kiwanis).
- ❏ Consider running for your local city council. Getting to know people active in your community can provide you with excellent resources for business as well as personal use.
- ❏ Write articles relating to your area of expertise and submit them for publication in industry journals and/or the business section of local newspapers.
- ❏ Find a non-profit organization in which you believe and that can benefit from your skills and contacts. Put yourself up for consideration as a member of their board of directors.
- ❏ Keep up with industry trends by reading journals. Not only will you be well informed, you'll have a variety of topics to discuss while networking.
- ❏ Find ways to connect with your counterparts in other companies. While you obviously don't want to give away company secrets or promising prospects, chances are you can find some ways to collaborate rather than compete head to head.

Self-Check:

1. What activities are you currently using for networking in your industry? If the payback has not been worthwhile, is it because you've been only minimally involved? If so, how can you become more involved? If you *have* been genuinely active, what other venues can you explore to replace the ineffective networking activities?
2. Do you belong to any organizations in which you're a member in name only? If so, either commit to more active involvement or drop the membership completely.
3. If you're currently not doing anything beyond your day-to-day tasks, choose something from the above list and commit to active involvement as a way of building your base of networking contacts. As always, when deciding about memberships, balance your investment of time and money against potential reward.

THE BOTTOM LINE:

1. Even if you're currently in your dream job, active and effective networking will increase your visibility and credibility within your own company and within your industry.
2. Having made solid contacts in your industry can come in very useful some day, just in case the dream becomes more of a nightmare.

Networking for a Move to a New Industry   11

You've heard the saying that the only certain things in life are death and taxes. While this is not the most optimistic perspective in the world, it does contain some truth. A dream position can become the job from hell if the new manager and you don't see eye to eye. You may burn out after years of intense effort. Or some day you may simply find yourself ready to spread your wings and try something new. It's at times like these that you'll be particularly glad to have invested time and effort in becoming active in various networking organizations, because you'll already have a good contact base established. (This is what CEO and author Harvey Mackay refers to as "digging your well before you're thirsty.") When it comes time to find a great new position, effective networking will be a powerful tool.

The Experienced Job-Seeker's One-Minute Commercial

Every commercial has the same purpose: to tell your listeners just enough about what you do that they're eager to learn more. When preparing your commercial for finding a new position, there are a few additional things to keep in mind:

- ❏ Keep the tone positive, even (or especially) if your leave-taking from your previous job was not pleasant.
- ❏ Emphasize your problem-solving abilities and transferable skills—those attributes that are applicable and valuable regardless of industry.

- ❑ Be willing to ask for exactly the type of contact you want, whether it's at a specific company, in a certain industry, or with an organization of a particular size.
- ❑ Throw modesty (but not accuracy) out the window. Tell people *exactly why* you'll be an asset to any employer. Back up these assertions with hard statistics whenever possible.
- ❑ Take advantage of any outplacement services offered to you. That way, if you're feeling less than positive about your past accomplishments, you'll have a professional available to help you identify them so you can include them in your commercial.
- ❑ Keep in mind that job titles can vary widely from one company to the next, and be especially careful not to pigeonhole yourself by leading with your title.

With these further guidelines in mind, you can use questions to generate the raw data that will help your listeners easily answer the question, *"What's in it for me* to refer or hire this person?"

- ❑ What kind of *problems* have I demonstrably solved in my previous positions? What sort of quantifiable results can I provide to prove the effectiveness of my problem solving?
- ❑ What kind of *pain* could an employer avoid by hiring me instead of someone else for a position?
- ❑ What have employers and customers (both internal and external) *appreciated* most about my work to date?
- ❑ I'm experienced in_____. *So what?* In other words, how will this experience *benefit* my new employer?
- ❑ What can I *save* for my employer? (For example, if you're skilled at creating a committed and effective team, you'll save her high turnover costs.)
- ❑ How can I help my employer *grow* her business/improve her bottom line? (This is a *great* time to haul out any statistics that demonstrate your ability to decrease expenses or increase revenues.)
- ❑ Why is hiring and working with me *easy* and *low risk?*

Self-Check:
1. Do you already have a commercial prepared for your search? If so, how does it stack up in terms of the tone, focus on employer benefits, and so forth?
2. If you're working on your commercial, what sort of answers are you developing for the questions listed above? Are your answers succinct? Focused on answering the WIIFM question for listeners? Accurate? Enticing? If not, how can your answers be improved?

Make the Most of Informational Interviewing to Expand Your Horizons

As discussed in chapter 9, Networking for New College Graduates, gathering information about an industry or company *before* accepting an offer can save a lot of heartache and energy. While you, as an experienced business professional, have an advantage over a recent college grad due to your far larger base of contacts, you too can get ideas about potential new positions through informational interviewing. Because of that larger base, you might want to use a standardized form for keeping track of your contacts; see appendix C for a sample data sheet.

Other Sources for Researching New Industries

- ❑ One of my favorite options is to use the services of information specialists at the large county libraries where I live. These wonder workers are highly trained and experienced at finding requested information quickly. While you may be well able to handle Internet searches yourself, why not take advantage of the specialized knowledge these library wizards have? It may turn out that they can promptly point you to a website or hard copy resource that you never knew existed. They can certainly help you track down a wide variety of resources.

- ❑ You may have identified a particular company as a leader in its industry. In this case, checking out the corporate website may give you a good overview of the industry as well as the specific company.

NET PROFIT

- ❏ Search for industry-specific publications. Read through them to get a feel for the industry.
- ❏ Identify the professional association associated with the industry and connect with its local chapter. See if you can attend a meeting as a guest and get first-hand industry information from people actively employed in the field. Do an online search to locate a directory of associations in the local area. Your state may have a resource very similar to the *Directory of Minnesota Business and Professional Associations,* which I've used with great success to identify useful organizations.
- ❏ Read the *Wall Street Journal* or other business newspapers. Remember to pay close attention to the business section of your local paper, as well.
- ❏ Consider subscribing to a local business publication. In the Twin Cities, the *Minneapolis/St. Paul Business Journal* provides information on a variety of local businesses and industries.

Self-Check:
1. Are you open to exploring a variety of new industries, or do you want to focus on a particular one?
2. What sources can you use to gather information on this new industry? Be specific.
3. Have you developed a list of questions to ask in informational interviews?

THE BOTTOM LINE:

1. A compelling and effective one-minute commercial will be a great help in looking for a position in a new industry. Take the time to craft an outstanding one.
2. Don't be shy about asking for help from the network of contacts you've diligently established in your previous positions. Remember, the majority of people will be flattered and very willing to help if you just ask them.

Networking for Your Own Business 12

More and more business professionals are opting for self-employment. Whether you make this choice because of burnout, downsizing, or a desire for something different, networking will be essential to your ongoing success.

What Can Business Owners Use Networking For?

A better question might be, "What *can't* you use it for?" because networking is a very versatile tool. Use it to find new

- ❑ prospects and clients;
- ❑ vendors;
- ❑ information resources;
- ❑ businesses with whom you can cross-market goods and services.

Whatever the goal of your networking, remember that *giving* in a networking relationship is at least as important as getting, and that it's vital to have a good answer to your listener's unspoken question, *"What's in it for me?"*

Prospects and Clients

In the movie *Jerry Maguire*, Tom Cruise plays a sports agent who pleads with his one and only client, "Help me help you." Turned around, this can help you make the most of your networking. Ask yourself what you can do to make it easy for your listener to help you. If someone's interested enough to ask you to describe your ideal prospect, you're missing a golden opportunity if you reply, in effect, "Anyone who can fog a mirror." This description is too vague to get anyone thinking. On the other hand, if you say something like, "I'm looking for owners of service businesses with twenty-five or fewer employees who market exclusively to other businesses," people can easily compare this description with people they know and, one hopes, come up with a match for you.

Leon provides a good example of effectively crafting a commercial and delivering it to the right audience. As president of a company providing Internet services to apartment complexes, he's identified his local builders' association as a great place to meet apartment managers and builders. His one-minute commercial emphasizes the cost-effectiveness of hiring his company as the ISP for the complex, so that the building owners can profitably provide Internet services as part of their tenants' monthly rent.

Vendors

Looking for a new service provider for your own company is perhaps one of the easiest applications of networking. Asking, "Who does your _____ for you? Are you pleased with them? Can I get their name?" may be all you need to get great referrals to someone who will be part of your business success.

Information Resources

People, the Internet, and libraries can all provide important information. Since the trick is to be as efficient and effective as possible in using these resources, be very clear in your own mind what *type* of information you're looking for. Is it specific data, contact information, background? Once you know exactly what you're looking for, you're ready to use your network of contacts to ensure you spend your time wisely. Any of the following questions can quickly set you on the right path:

- ❏ "I'm looking for information on _____ and I'm not sure where to start. Do you know anyone who has dealt with this situation?"
- ❏ "Do you know of any websites that provide information on _____?"
- ❏ "When you were dealing with _____, who did you go to for help?"

Cross-marketing Partners

Look for businesses whose products and services *complement* yours and are geared toward the same target market. You can be a highly valuable resource for such companies—and vice versa—for numerous reasons:

- Each of you can provide access to contacts in your data base that are not in the other's.

- You can make your clients' lives easier by saying, "If you need help with [name your partner's area of expertise], I know someone I can refer to you." This naturally makes you even more valuable as a problem-solver to your clients.

- You can serve as subcontractors for one another. You're likely to encounter situations where you alone can't provide all the services a client needs. You can still get the job by subcontracting with someone with the complementary skills you lack. She can charge you her usual rates, which you mark up (think of it as a finder's fee) before including in your bill to the client. The client's needs are met with no additional effort on her part, and both you and your partner earn revenue you might not have otherwise had access to.

An example of this is seen in the way Lauri and Sharron work together. Lauri is an outstanding marketing consultant; Sharron has vast experience in publishing and a well developed publishing niche. As is common in the industry, Sharron relies on authors to develop most of the ideas for marketing their books. When Sharron has a client who needs marketing assistance, she can refer the author to Lauri for help in that area. By the same token, if the marketing plan developed by Lauri and her client calls for writing and publishing a book, Lauri can send that prospect to Sharron.

- If subcontracting is for some reason not feasible, you can still add to each other's bottom lines with referral or finder's fees.

- You can co-sponsor programs and events with your marketing partner, thus reducing individual costs while both of you get your names into the marketplace.

- You have a built-in brainstorming partner who can help develop new strategies, contacts, even products or services.

Following are examples of potentially valuable cross-marketing partnerships:

- CPA and business attorney
- real estate agent and mortgage broker
- web designer and print designer
- financial planner and estate planning attorney
- interior designer and painter who does faux finishes on walls
- promotional products company and marketing strategist
- stained glass artist and architects or builders of high-end homes.

Self-Check:

1. How do you currently describe your ideal prospective client? If the description lacks enough specificity to paint a clear picture, revise it so as to make it easier for your listener to say, "I know the exact person you're looking for."
2. What type of vendor do you or will you have need of? Do you have any requirements in terms of size, specialty, geographic location, and so forth?
3. Is there any specific information you're currently looking for? If so, what? The more clearly you can identify what you need, the easier you make it on yourself and on those people you ask for help.
4. Think of your target market. What other products or services do members of this group need? Which of these products and services are a good complement for what you offer?
5. What compelling arguments can you make when suggesting a cross-marketing partnership to another business owner?

Networking or Leads-Passing Groups

Many business owners looking for new clients find it useful to join a group specifically dedicated to passing high-quality referrals among group members. While the structure and cost of such groups vary, they typically have several characteristics in common:

- They meet weekly or bi-weekly at the same time and place.

NETWORKING FOR YOUR OWN BUSINESS

- ❏ Membership is on a non-compete basis; in other words, only one representative from any given business/industry is allowed in the group.
- ❏ Each member gets to give her one-minute commercial at each meeting; this allows everyone to become familiar and comfortable with fellow members' businesses.
- ❏ Typically at each meeting one group member will get anywhere from ten to twenty minutes to describe her business in greater detail; sometimes the group will bring in an outside speaker to provide an educational mini-seminar.
- ❏ Costs typically include monthly dues and sometimes an initial application fee, as well, especially for networking organizations with a national presence.
- ❏ You're either required or strongly encouraged to belong to only *one* referral group. In this way, there's no conflict in figuring out which real estate agent from your seven leads groups gets your referral.

You'll find both proponents and opponents of leads-passing groups. Here are some pros and cons to consider. On the plus side:

- ❏ Everyone in the group is there for the express purpose of giving and receiving leads, so there's no need to be shy about asking for what you want.
- ❏ You meet with fellow group members frequently, so you have the chance to share various aspects of your business with them. This helps them more effectively connect you with the type of prospect you're seeking.
- ❏ The group provides a safe place for experimenting with new versions of your commercial and getting feedback on them.
- ❏ You're only one step (one degree of separation) away from all the people in your fellow members' circles of contacts, which effectively increases your network by many times.

On the negative side of the ledger:

- ❏ The slots for certain professions (e.g., real estate, financial planning, insurance, and so forth) fill quickly in referral groups, so you may have trouble finding a group in which your business is not already represented.

- ❏ Initiation and monthly fees may be relatively high.
- ❏ The groups require a serious commitment of time and energy.
- ❏ The composition of the group may change over time to a mix of businesses that's not a good fit for you.
- ❏ The leads given are sometimes not well thought out or well matched to your needs, but rather are given solely to meet expectations of giving referrals.

If, after you've considered these points, you feel you want to join a group, how do you go about finding one? There are several ways to do so:

- ❏ Ask around your circle of contacts.
- ❏ Check the calendar in the business section of local newspapers. Typically this will list the meeting times and venues of a variety of networking groups.
- ❏ Do an Internet search on "business networking," "referral groups," and "leads groups" to find national organizations that might have chapters in your area.
- ❏ Check with your local Chamber of Commerce (you *have* joined your local Chamber, right?) to find out if they sponsor or know of any such groups.

Okay, so you have a list of possible groups to join. Since you'll want to choose only one of these groups, how do you decide which one will best meet your needs? Answers to the following questions will help:

- ❏ Is there an opening in the group for the business I represent?
- ❏ Do I need a group with strictly B2B members, or is a mixed group of B2B and B2C businesses better for me? What's the make-up of this particular group I'm considering?
- ❏ When and where do they meet?
- ❏ What are the monthly and annual costs, if any?
- ❏ Are there any requirements in terms of number of referrals I'm expected to pass to fellow group members?
- ❏ Does the group allow me to visit one or more times as a guest, so I can get a feel for whether it's a good fit for me and vice versa?
- ❏ How long has this group/chapter been in existence?

❑ What sort of statistics can they provide on number of referrals passed and the dollar value of the actual business generated through these leads?

Self-Check:
1. Have you identified groups you're eligible to join?
2. Have you invited yourself to a meeting of each group yet?
3. Are you willing to spend the money and are you firmly committed to spend the time required to participate in this group?
4. Do you clearly understand that you have a responsibility to *actively* look for appropriate referrals for fellow group members? Are you willing to meet this ongoing responsibility?

THE BOTTOM LINE:
1. Be clear and explicit when asking for contacts of any sort.
2. Be creative when identifying the type of person whom you can help and who can help you.
3. Thank everyone who connects you with a useful resource, both verbally and with a handwritten note.
4. Be thorough in evaluating the potential value of any specific leads-passing group.
5. If you do elect to join such a group, commit to active participation in it.

Networking at Business Expos and Trade Shows 13

Whether you work for a corporation or for yourself, chances are good that at some point you'll be called upon to represent your company at a trade show or business expo. While most of the preceding chapters' suggestions and techniques can be used to advantage at expos, these venues require additional networking skills in order for you to make the most of the opportunities they present.

Managing Time

The very first chance you'll have to manage time well is when registering for exhibit space at a trade show or business expo. Not only will signing up in a timely manner typically entitle you to an early bird discount on the cost of your exhibit space, it will also assure you the best choice of spaces (see Managing Logistics later in this chapter for more on location).

While a business expo is very different from other networking events, arriving early is still one of the most helpful things you can do to make the expo productive.

❑ In those rare cases where you're not given a chance to reserve a specific spot ahead of time, exhibitors' tables within the expo hall may be assigned on a first-come, first-served basis. Arriving early assures that you get a prime location.

NET PROFIT

- ❑ If the venue for the event has limited parking, you don't want to get stuck parking rather far from the entrance to the exhibit hall. Giving yourself plenty of travel time allows you to calmly find a convenient parking space and leisurely move your materials to your table.
- ❑ You'll be ready to connect with even the earliest arriving attendees.
- ❑ You'll have a chance to either offer help to or request help from fellow exhibitors also setting up their booths.
- ❑ Once your exhibit is set up and arranged effectively, you're free to check out the rest of the event and talk to fellow exhibitors (who are, after all, also potential clients, vendors, or marketing partners).

Another aspect of managing time at a business expo has to do with spending enough time speaking to each prospect without tying yourself up for too long a time with any one visitor to your booth. It'll help to remember you're *not* looking to make a sale right at the expo. You're seeking to establish a point of common interest and to set the stage for a follow-up meeting at a later date, at which time you can determine whether you're the problem-solver of her dreams. See Managing Personal Interactions later in this chapter for more tips on finding the balance between too much time and not enough.

Although it's not a happy thought to contemplate, chances are excellent that, at some point or another, you'll be at an expo raring to go, and no one is stopping at your booth. There are a few things you can do to make this dead time more bearable.

- ❑ Work the booth with someone else. This could be a trusted employee, your business partner, or even a satisfied client. You'll always have someone to talk to, which helps keep your energy up.
- ❑ Take advantage of slow times to connect with exhibitors at adjacent booths; perhaps you can be of service to each other down the road.
- ❑ Make notes about specific actions you'll take to follow up with previous visitors to your booth.
- ❑ Definitely *resist* the temptation to make the time go more quickly by talking on your cell phone, even if it's to a client. This is almost a sure-fire way to guarantee your perfect prospect will come along

NETWORKING AT BUSINESS EXPOS AND TRADE SHOWS

and, seeing you're on the phone, pass by without stopping. In fact, turn your cell phone off so there's no chance of it being a distraction.

> **Self-Check:**
> 1. When do you typically register for a business expo—right away, at the last minute, or somewhere in between? Can you make it a point to be more prompt about this task?
> 2. How much time do you need to leisurely set up your display booth and materials? For any given expo, how much travel time do you need to allow in order to have adequate set-up time?

Managing Logistics

Trade shows and business expos are interesting beasts. They definitely count as work, yet they're typically more casual than many other business activities. They require a high level of energy and involvement, yet often make an exhibitor feel like she's done her job simply by showing up and staffing the booth. They're designed to encourage interactions, but the very fact that there's a table available can make it easy to hide behind it. How do you strike a balance between formal and casual, involved and aggressive, comfortable and accessible? Here are some handy Do's and Don'ts.

DO:

- ❏ whatever is necessary to get an exhibit space in a high-traffic area, whether that means spending extra money or signing up early or both. Some exhibitors swear by the end cap position, i.e., the table placed at the end of a row of tables and perpendicular to them. Others prefer to have a booth near the buffet table, so anyone wanting food will have to spend some time in front of the booth, too. Still others prefer the spot nearest the entry.
- ❏ if a certain expo is held on an ongoing basis, consider going once or twice as an attendee before shelling out the money to be an exhibitor. Observe the traffic flow and density and use this information to choose the space you'll select for your own exhibit at the next expo put on by that organization.

NET PROFIT

- ❏ invest in a good quality display, if you plan to exhibit at trade shows or expos on a regular basis (a cardboard or hand lettered sign definitely does *not* create an image of professionalism or competence). Also, it's well worth the money to buy lights with your display. Not only are event venues often poorly lit, but few of your fellow exhibitors will have lights. Good focused lighting, combined with an attractive display, does a great job of enticing people to stop by and talk.
- ❏ create a list of materials that you want to take to the expo. Review your expo inventory against this list *before* leaving for the event and re-stock as needed. It's *really* embarrassing to realize you've run out of information when you're talking to someone you want to impress with your competence and professionalism.
- ❏ *stand* at your booth, even if a chair is provided; sitting makes you look disengaged and disinterested. If the event runs more than a couple of hours, consider investing in a rubber floor mat (like the ones used by supermarket cashiers) to make standing more comfortable.
- ❏ stand in front of the table or off to one side of it, never behind. Stationing yourself behind the table makes it more difficult to physically connect with potential visitors, creates a psychological barrier between you and the people you're there to meet, and implies you lack confidence and business savvy.
- ❏ turn your cell phone off unless there's a *truly* compelling reason to have it on (for example, you're waiting to hear how your mom came though her open-heart surgery). Note: Wanting to stay in touch does *not* count as sufficiently important.

DON'T:

- ❏ eat at your booth. Doing so looks unprofessional, leads to messy handshakes, and causes you to run the risk of talking to an important prospect with poppyseeds between your teeth. Much better to eat either before or after the event.
- ❏ drink alcohol at your booth, no matter how many of your fellow exhibitors are doing it. While some prospects may find that perfectly acceptable, there will almost certainly be others who

consider it unprofessional. In a situation like this, it pays to be conservative; limit your liquid refreshment to water while the event is in progress. Afterwards, if you like, you can celebrate all the great leads you developed with a glass of wine.

❑ bring a bunch of literature, lay it flat on the table, and consider your display complete. Paper is just not exciting. You need interesting graphics or props to grab people's attention long enough for you to connect with them. Balloons, useful promotional products, an interactive CD presentation on your laptop, a door-prize drawing, and the always-popular free food can all attract a visitor's attention long enough to give you a chance to start a conversation with her.

Self-Check:

1. Do you consciously choose an advantageous position for your exhibit, or is the choice more hit-or-miss?
2. Do you typically stand or sit at your booth? And where do you do this (i.e., in front of or behind the table)?
3. Do you eat or drink anything while exhibiting?
4. Is your cell phone typically on or off?
5. Is your booth physically attractive and eye-catching? If it's on the sluggish side, what can you do to liven it up?

Managing Personal Interactions

Business expos attendees see a wide array of behaviors by the exhibitors, from dynamic to insipid, effective to off-putting, and everything in between. The goal for you, as an exhibitor, is to demonstrate that you're a valuable business professional who's worth spending more time with. See which of the following strategies you're already using:

❑ Expect the best. A friendly and optimistic demeanor can do a lot to attract people to your booth and give you a chance to establish some contact with them.

❑ Smile! It's amazing how grim some people can look and how much of a turn-off that can be.

- ❑ Be willing to be playful. If you enjoy what you do and bring a lot of energy to your work, let visitors to your booth know that. After all, what prospect wouldn't want a creative, energetic, hard-working professional on her side? Lauri, a marketing strategist, has been known to sing to expo visitors, often with the help of satisfied clients who have stopped by her booth to say, "Hi."

- ❑ Be ready to reach out to people with a genuine greeting. A plain old "Hello" doesn't do much to start any type of meaningful conversation. Instead, add an open-ended question and see how far that gets you. For example, something like, "Hi! What sort of interesting things have you seen here so far?" invites discussion.

- ❑ While focusing on your current conversational partner, stay at least peripherally aware of any other visitors who approach while you're speaking. You can look at them briefly to include them in your remarks, then bring your main focus back to your first guest. This shows respect for your original visitor, other prospects looking for information, and yourself as a business representative seeking to make as many good contacts as possible.

- ❑ Resist the temptation to strong-arm people into stopping at your booth, even—or especially—if the event has been a little slow. You don't want to develop a reputation for aggressively cornering people. Even if you lure someone into a conversation, the pressure tactics are likely to be such a turn-off that the prospect will be unwilling to hear or seriously consider what you have to say.

- ❑ If someone is starting to monopolize your time, pull out a stock phrase you've developed prior to the event and use this to extricate yourself without alienating the person who was so interested to begin with. Use or modify one of the following:

    - ✔ "It sounds like there's quite a bit more for us to discuss. Shall we get together over coffee later this week to talk some more?"
    - ✔ "I'd like the chance to discuss this in a quieter setting. May I e-mail (or call) you to set up a time when we can talk more comfortably?"
    - ✔ "It looks like I have questions to answer for some other people. Can we get together later to continue this talk?"

❏ Promptly follow-up. It's been estimated that as many as *80 percent* of trade show leads are never contacted after the show. When you quickly (i.e., within forty-eight hours maximum) do whatever you said you would do, you demonstrate your integrity, reliability, and professionalism. Take pains to be prompt with follow-up whether or not the prospect is currently a hot lead. Strongly consider sending handwritten thank you notes to those who stopped by your booth and spent some time with you.

Self-Check:

1. What's your general attitude toward exhibiting at expos? Can it use a tune-up?
2. What sort of greeting do you typically use at expos? Can you think of some open-ended questions to ask attendees that will allow you to start a conversation with them?
3. Have you had problems in the past with getting tied up with one particular visitor to your booth? How did you extricate yourself? Can you benefit from new strategies for wrapping up one conversation so you can move on to the next?

THE BOTTOM LINE:

1. A trade show or business expo can either be highly productive or a big waste of time and money. Your level of preparation for the event does much to determine your probable outcome.
2. Consider attending expos before exhibiting at them. Note effective and ineffective displays, behaviors, set-ups; commit to emulating the former and avoiding the latter.

Pulling it All Together

14

At this point you've probably spent a goodly amount of time assessing and polishing your networking skills. The key now is to *practice* these as often as you can, so that you become unconsciously competent in their use.

Remember the NQ assessment in chapter 1 that addressed Ten Top Networking Oopses? Here's a list of those critical mistakes, in all their unproductive glory. Starting with number ten, they're ranked in increasing order of importance *and* of challenge when it comes to making changes. Which corrections will yield the greatest dividends for you?

The Top Ten Networking Oopses

10. Limp handshake.
9. Inconsistent attendance at events and/or chronic late arrivals.
8. Hanging out only with people you already know.
7. Being passive, waiting for someone else to make the first introduction.
6. Being blah/low energy.
5. Trying to be too many things to too many prospects/lacking focus on a target market.
4. Failing to ask for help in getting what you need.

3. Not having any specific goals for a given event; being mentally unprepared.
2. Leading with your job title or list of services.
1. Being a taker and a talker more than a giver and a listener.

And, as a special added bonus:
Failing to follow up promptly and effectively.

There's a quick reference sheet in appendix D that summarizes the differences between networking that's blah versus brilliant. Feel free to use it as a handy review or reminder of those areas you want most to work on.

What's great about networking is that, done well, it's satisfying, productive, profitable, and just plain fun. I hope you've gleaned some ideas that will make your networking activities even more valuable to you. I'd love to hear your success stories; please send them to me at kath@yourclientconnection.com so I can share them with others. (Please note that all submissions become the property of Client Connections and may be used in future publications.)

Appendix A

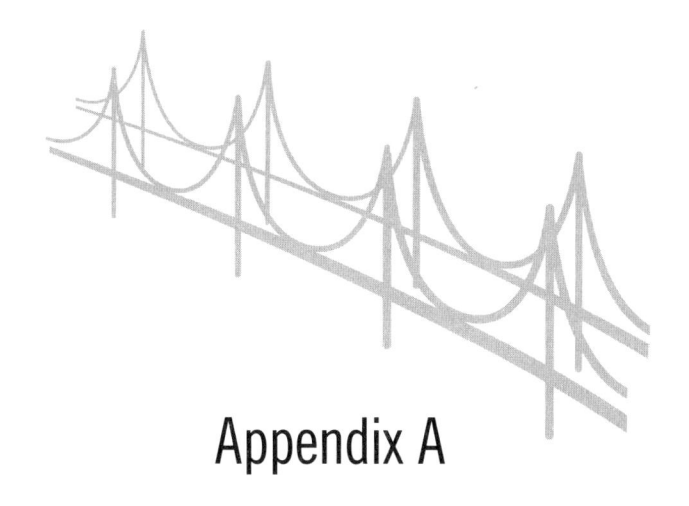

Scoring Your NQ Self-Assessment

Here are the responses indicative of an outstanding networker.

1. How do people tend to react to your handshake?
   a. with a warm smile and interest

2. What do you see the most of when speaking to someone at a networking event?
   c. the face of the person you're speaking with

3. What type of comment do you hear most frequently at networking events?
   b. "Wow! It seems I see you everywhere I go."

4. Say you've spoken with someone several times before at previous networking events. If she were to introduce you and your business to a third party, what would she say?
   c. she'd confidently and energetically share your name, your company name, and a brief one-liner describing the work you do

5. What's your most typical behavior when entering a networking event?
   b. seek out a friendly new face and introduce yourself

NET PROFIT

6. How would someone describe your conversational style at networking events?
    b. "Boy, she's a great listener."
7. What do you consider an appropriate way to ask for help in making a particular kind of contact?
    c. "I'm looking for a connection to someone who _____. Do you know anyone like that? Would you be comfortable introducing me to them?"
8. What do you typically want to accomplish at a networking event?
    a. to make one or more contacts for a new potential client or strategic partner *and* to give one or more referrals
9. When you introduce yourself, what information—other than your name and that of your business—do you share?
    c. a brief statement of the sort of problems you solve for your clients
10. What best describes your attitude toward networking events?
    b. it's an exciting way to make connections that will benefit others as well as yourself

Scores:

0-5: do yourself a favor and make it a priority to practice everything in this book

6-8: feel good about what you're already doing well and about knowing areas where you can become more effective

9-10: pat yourself on the back and strongly consider offering classes that teach others how to network effectively

Appendix B

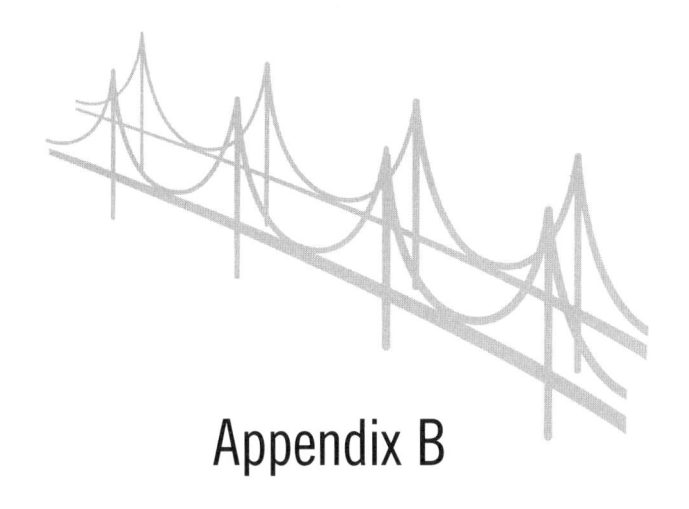

Questions for Evaluating Prospective Membership Groups

- ❑ What types of people typically join this organization?
- ❑ What sort of contacts am I looking to make? Prospective new clients? Referral sources? Potential strategic partners?
- ❑ If I operate multiple businesses or have a multi-faceted primary business, on which specific venture will I focus this networking?
- ❑ For B2B, or *business-to-business* service providers: Am I looking for small-business owners or executives in larger corporations? What size company is an ideal prospect for me in terms of revenues, number of employees, or other useful criteria? Am I looking to connect with start-up, young, or established businesses?
- ❑ For B2C, or *business-to-consumer* service providers: What are the demographics and/or psychographics of my ideal prospect? (*Note:* "Everyone" is not a useful way to describe your target market!)
- ❑ Is there a match between the existing membership and the types of contacts I'm seeking?
- ❑ Does the membership include people who also serve my target market, although in some complementary field? (For example, a business attorney might seek contact with CPA's because they both specialize in small-to-medium businesses; their services are related, not competitive.)

- ❏ Is the primary purpose of the group to provide community service? Networking for business-building purposes? Support for a particular cause? Something else?
- ❏ Which of these goals is most in line with what I want to get out of my membership?
- ❏ What specific opportunities exist for becoming active in the organization? Ongoing events? Committees? Leadership roles?
- ❏ How much does it cost to join and participate? Annual dues? Program fees? Other costs?
- ❏ How much time and money am I willing to invest in networking in this organization?
- ❏ Would I feel good about being associated with these people and this group? Is the chemistry good?
- ❏ What do existing members have to say about the organization? How long have they been members? How has the group met their needs? What do they consider the three greatest benefits about their membership? What activities have they found to be most valuable to them, and why? What group activities/procedures would they change if they could?
- ❏ On a scale of 1 to 10, with 1 being totally not worthwhile and 10 being this is a perfect fit for me, how does this organization rate?

Appendix C

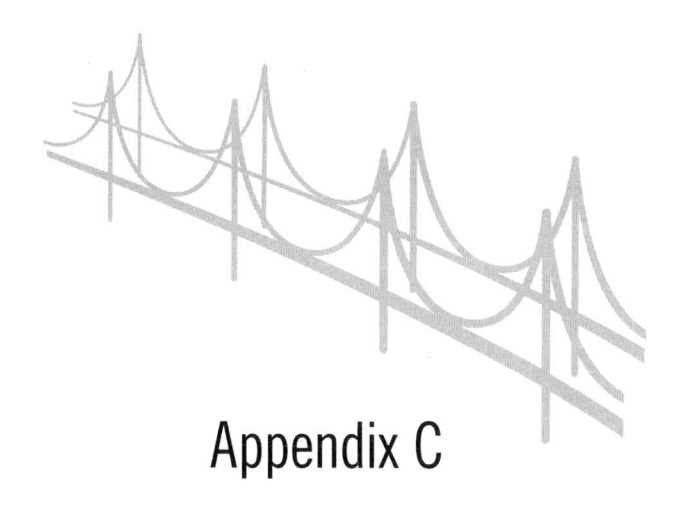

Informational Interview Data Sheet

Company name and address:

Contact person (name, title, phone, etc.):

Who referred me to this contact person? When? Why?

History of contacts (letter sent, voicemail message left, etc.):

Date and time of interview:

Directions to meeting venue printed out?

Date thank you note sent:

Appendix D

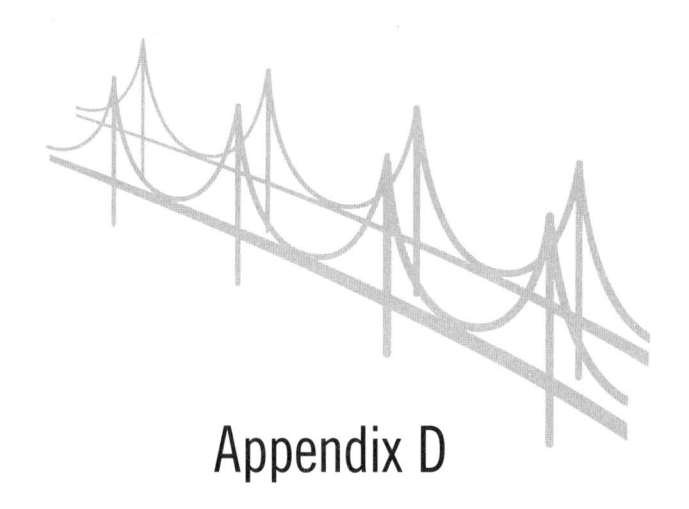

The Difference Between Blah and Brilliant

Whereas an ineffective networker will	an effective one will
have a dead-fish handshake (Oops #10)	• make sure there's solid contact between her web of skin (between thumb and forefinger) and the other person's web
attend events now and then (Oops #9)	• choose events providing the highest return on investment of time and money, then attend them consistently • schedule these events in her planner and make attendance a priority
arrive late (Oops #9)	• arrive early to scope out the room set up, name tags of attendees, etc. • become the center of a small group of people so she doesn't have to break into an established conversation

Whereas an ineffective networker will	an effective one will
hang out with people she already knows (Oops #8)	• expand her comfort zone by deliberately seeking out new faces • ensure that at least one new person is on either side of her when sitting down for a meal
act like a guest (Oops #7)	• act like a host: introduce herself to people, then introduce them to newcomers (this builds confidence, makes her memorable, and makes her the shy person's hero)
be blah (Oops #6)	• choose an energetic, positive attitude • be genuine • be here now
lack focus (Oops #5)	• identify, in advance, her core competency (i.e., what she does *best*) and how that provides solutions for the listener's problems • refuse to try being all things to all people
assume listeners know what she needs or wants (Oops #4)	• clearly ask for the type of contact or referral she needs
lack goals for any given event (Oops #3)	• know if she wants a contact in a particular company or industry, or a certain type of potential strategic ally • have goals related to *giving* as well as getting

APPENDIX D

Whereas an ineffective networker will	an effective one will
wing it (Oops #3)	• have a carefully prepared one-minute commercial ready so she can quickly describe the *benefits* of doing business with her • have questions ready that can be used to start an interesting dialogue • have escape-hatch phrases prepared so that she can easily move from one conversation to another • practice these in a safe environment (e.g., a Chamber seminar on networking)
give an inconsistent message (Oops #3)	• know the bottom-line benefits she offers clients and reiterate these consistently • discuss different aspects of her business while still focusing on the same type of benefits provided
lead with her title or a laundry list of services (Oops #2)	• briefly describe the *concept* of her business • show how she provides solutions to clients' (or prospects') problems • show the prospect what's in it for *them*
talk and tell, talk and tell, talk and tell… (Oops #1)	• give the other person a chance to talk first • truly *listen* to the other person's comments • remember that "a brilliant conversationalist is one who talks to you about yourself" (Lisa Kirk)

85

Whereas an ineffective networker will	an effective one will
only be interested in what she can get from the other person (Oops #1)	• focus energy on identifying how she can serve as a resource to the other person • ask herself, "How can *I* help this person? What can I give *her*?"
ask only yes/no questions, if any (Oops #1)	• ask open-ended questions to engage the other person • remember that "the opposite of talking isn't listening; the opposite of talking is waiting" (Fran Lebowitz)
trust her good memory for follow-up (Bonus Oops)	• take notes on the other person's business cards, comments as well as action to be taken, *if* she's doing business in a country and culture where this is considered acceptable practice
fail to follow-up (Bonus Oops)	• use some sort of system to create a method of staying in future contact with good prospects or potential allies • *commit* to prompt follow-up, actually scheduling time for it in her planner

Appendix E

Additional Resources

Gerber, Michael. *The E-Myth Revisited*. New York: Harper-Collins, 2001.

Hall, Edward T. *The Silent Language*. New York: Anchor Books, 1990.

Mackay, Harvey. *Dig Your Well Before You're Thirsty: The Only Networking Book You'll Ever Need*. New York: Doubleday, 1997.

Mehrabian, Albert. *Nonverbal Communication*. Chicago: Aldine Atherton, 1972.

Continuing education seminars offered through universities, local chapters of national professional associations, etc.

www.act.com provides information on purchasing and using ACT!, a popular customer relationship management (CRM) software program. It also can connect you with local certified ACT! consultants who can help you get a quick start on using the software effectively.

www.bni.com is the website for Business Network International, a large leads-passing organization with a global presence; it can direct you to local chapters.

www.cardscan.com will introduce you to some of the most popular business card scanners on the market. You'll find one that's easy to use and suitable for your needs.

www.entrepreneur.com is a website geared toward the myriad facets of being a successful business owner.

www.frontrange.com is the corporate site for the makers of GoldMine, another popular CRM software option. They offer an entire suite of related products to make your contact management easier.

About the Author

Kathleen Watson is the founder and principal of Client Connections, a business matchmaking company helping clients develop valuable relationships that grow their businesses. Her clients appreciate her skills as an energetic, enthusiastic, see-her-everywhere advocate.

Kathleen has a long history of being a "go to" person and for over twenty years has served as a valuable information resource in the fields of sales, marketing, and education.

After receiving her MBA, with an emphasis in marketing, from the University of Minnesota, she started her own training company, specializing in helping people to become more powerful communicators.

In her eight years as an instructor for Minnesota State Colleges and Universities, she helped hundreds of adult learners assess their educational and career goals and identify the best educational path to meet those goals.

A firm believer in the value of connecting with others both professionally and personally, Kathleen is an award-winning member of several Chambers of Commerce, donates both time and money to nonprofit (social profit) organizations serving the disadvantaged, and was privileged to take part in the 2006 international Quest for Global Healing Conference in Bali.

She lives with her husband, Joseph, and two golden retrievers in Minneapolis, Minnesota.